Gonna take a sentimental journey,
Gonna set my heart at ease.
Gonna make a sentimental journey,
To renew old memories.

Seven, that's the time we leave, at seven.
I'll be waitin' up for heaven,
Countin' every mile of railroad track
That takes me back.

Got my bag, I got my reservation,
Spent each dime I could afford.
Like to hear that **_All Aboard!_**

ALL ABOARD!

THE GOLDEN AGE OF
AMERICAN RAIL TRAVEL

Edited by Bill Yenne

BARNES
&NOBLE
BOOKS
NEW YORK

4

This edition published by Barnes & Noble Inc.
by arrangement with Brompton Books Corporation.

Produced by Brompton Books Corporation
15 Sherwood Place
Greenwich, CT 06830

ISBN 0-88029-353-5

Printed in China
Reprinted 1990, 1993, 1995
Designed and edited by Bill Yenne
Captioned by Marie Cahill

Page one: A quotation from the song *Sentimental Journey* (words and music by Bud Green, Les Brown and Ben Homer). *Page three:* An image of happiness from a bygone era of the Pennsylvania Railroad from 1948. *Below:* Waiting for the Canadian Pacific at Vermillion Bay, Ontario on 18 August 1900.

TABLE OF CONTENTS

INTRODUCTION

By Bill Yenne

'All aboard!'

The words rose in a firm baritone that brought hoards of travelers hustling and bustling toward the heavy, solid stainless steel doorways that would soon close behind them. Six generations of Americans—enclosed within a Pullman car like a baby swaddled in a blanket—embarked upon a great adventure that was once a way of life, and today is no more.

'All aboard!'

He rarely had to repeat it. They were listening and they had heard him. He stood by, steadfast, patient, resplendent in his dark blue uniform, eyeing his gold pocket watch for the exact moment—the precise second—when he would make his announcement. The authority he possessed was to similar to that of a ship's captain, and he was one of the most respected figures in American life. He was the conductor.

'All aboard!'

For more than a century, the railroad conductor and his call were as much a part of the American scene as Monday night football or suburban shopping malls are today. No more. Though the words still echo down the cobbled and cracked concrete platforms across the land, the sentimental journey is indeed just an old memory. The passenger service of America's railroads began to face a serious challenge from airlines in about 1946, and by 1950 rail passenger service was the underdog. Many innovations were introduced on the rails in the 1950s, but the decade was the true twilight of the golden age. By the 1960s, with schedules drastically curtailed—or simply *not met*—the dream was over, the journey just a miserable parody of its former self.

Since it was formed in 1970 as the government-owned nationwide passenger service, the National Rail Passenger Corporation (Amtrak) has attempted to keep the dream alive, but it is a fact of life that most Americans simply no longer 'take the train.' The same is generally true in Canada, where most national passenger service was taken over by VIA in 1978.

Yet there is a profound fascination, a longing, for those days of magic and glory, when trains, like the *Broadway Limited*, the *Super Chief* and the *Coast Daylight*, were the last word in transportation. It was an era when airplanes were still unreliable and highways were torturous two-lane affairs unfit for a journey of more than a hundred miles. It was the time of the gleaming Pullman car, the conductor and his call. It was the golden age of American rail travel!

Above: A day in the life of an Amtrak passenger in the 1980s was little changed from that of Pennsy passengers *(right)* in the 1940s, but the route structure was a ghost of the sprawling network that once graced the North American continent. Schedules, too, now bear little resemblance to the past. Amtrak now runs fewer than a half dozen transcontinental routes, whereas in the golden age there were dozens. It's still service with a smile—if you have time to wait for a train!

7

STEEL ACROSS THE FRONTIER

FRONTIER

1869-1899

PART ONE

STEEL ACROSS THE FRONTIER

By Bill Yenne

The first commercial use of railroads to transport paying passengers came in 1830, but it was just as well to take a horse—or a horse-drawn conveyance. Stagecoaches could take you nearly anywhere, so railroads remained largely a novelty until 1850, by which time there were 9021 miles of rails, mostly in the Northeast.

In the early days, the railroads usually followed the lines of least resistance in laying their tracks. The railroads went by rote to such an extent that, according to tradition, the standard gauge—which is the inside distance between the rails—was determined by the width between the wheels of the ancient Roman chariots. Early English stagecoaches, according to the legend, were built to fit the grooves these chariots had made. When the first English railroads were constructed, the tracks were laid to the gauge of the stagecoaches, and the railroad cars and steam engines were built to fit that gauge.

Then, when the engines made in England were brought to America, the tracks were laid to match their gauge; and that is why, the story goes, the standard gauge in the United States is the odd figure of four feet, eight and a half inches.

Railroad building in the southern states had made little headway in the first half of the nineteenth century, and in the Midwest only three important lines were begun. In New England, where the country was the most densely populated, the progress was greater, so that by 1850 nearly all the important trunk lines in that region had been completed.

The ten years following 1850 were far more important in railroad history than the preceding decade. The increase between 1850 and 1860 was from 9021 to 30,635 miles, a result of several factors. The southern and midwestern states were developing, thereby creating a demand for greater transportation facilities. The discovery of gold in California in 1848 until 1857 brought the people of the United States highly prosperous times. Business activity in all lines was keen, and railroad building shared with other enterprises in this prosperity.

During the decade following 1850 many of the trunk lines of

Above: The dawning of the golden age of steam—in 1831, *John Bull*, the first steam locomotive in the US, was delivered from England. It arrived without assembly instructions, but mechanic Isaac Dripps solved the puzzle. *John Bull* provided passenger service for the Amboy & Camden, running the short distance between Bordertown and South Amboy. Within a generation, railroads would span the continent. *Below:* Today, *John Bull* can be seen at the Smithsonian Institution.

the large railroad systems of the present day were completed. The Erie Railroad joined New York with Lake Erie in 1851, and the Baltimore & Ohio reached the Ohio River the same year. The construction of long lines proceeded rapidly in the states east of the Mississippi River and north of the Ohio. By 1853 it became possible to travel from the Atlantic seaboard to Chicago by rail. In the following year, the Chicago & Rock Island connected Chicago with the Mississippi River. Land grants, state subsidies, and prosperous times combined to foster the rapid spread of the railroad net in the Midwest. This lasted until 1857, when the good times were interrupted by a panic. Railroad building was then so seriously interrupted that it had not regained its previous activity when the Civil War stopped nearly all industrial progress for half a decade.

Indeed, it was not until the golden spike was driven on 1 May 1869 at Promontory, Utah, that the nation was truly united. With that momentous event, a rail line stretched uninterrupted from San Francisco to Omaha, and then from Omaha to Chicago, where it connected to the already existing American rail network in the Northeast, the South and the vast industrial heartland around the Great Lakes.

With the completion of the transcontinental railroad, the golden age had begun.

*O*ne of the best accounts of American rail travel in the years before the Pullman era was related by an anonymous Englishman concerning his trip from Albany to Buffalo in 1861 on the New York Central.

The conductor, seeing him walk about the platform, eyeing the several carriages, asked with sagacious forethought, 'Sleeping car, mister? Going through, stranger?'

He replied, 'Yes,' and followed the quiet, sallow man into the last carriage, lettered in large red letters on a sunflower-yellow ground, *Albany and Buffalo Sleeping Car*.

'I go in and find an ordinary railway carriage; the usual filter, and the usual stove are there; and the seats,' said the traveler. 'Two and two, are arranged in the old quiet procession, turning their backs on each other glumly, after their kind. I ask how much extra I must pay for a bed.'

'Single-high, twenty-five cents; yes, sir,' said the conductor. 'Double-low, half a dollar; yes, sir.'

The traveler ordered a 'single-high' (without at all knowing what was meant), and as he paid his twenty-five cents, the bell on the engine begins to get restless, the steam horses snorted and champed and struggled. Ten other persons entered, and ordered beds and pay for themselves, with more or less expectation, regret and wrangling.

More bell, more steam, smothering them all with white—a wrench, a drag, a jolt back half angry, as if the engine were sulky and restive, and they were off. The signal posts and the timber yards flew by, and they were in the open country, with its zigzag snake fences, Indian corn patches and piles of orange pumpkins. Ladies came in from other carriages. (Unlike British trains of the period, a restless or seeking traveler could walk *through* the American train.)

Seated in twos and twos, some musing, some chatting, some discussing 'the irrepressible squabble,' many people were chewing or cutting plugs of tobacco from long wedges, produced from their waistcoat pockets. The candy boys came

Right: Western & Atlantic's *The General* was captured by Union soldiers during the Civil War. *The General's* conductor gave chase—first on foot, then on a push car, and finally on commandeered locomotives—and the soldiers abandoned the locomotive.

around three times and the man with the water can twice, while the lad with the book basket passed but once.

One hour from Albany they were at Hoffman's; twenty minutes more, at Amsterdam; fifty minutes more and they had reached Spraker's — pure Dutch names all, as though old Henry Hudson had christened them himself. Between Little Falls and Herkimer, the officer of the sleeping car entered, and called out:

'Now then, misters, if you please, get up from your seats, and allow me to make up the beds.'

Two by two they rose, and with neat trimness and quick hand the nimble Yankees turned over every other seat, so as to reverse the back, and make two seats, one facing the other. Nimbly they shut the windows and pulled up the shutters, leaving for ventilation the strip of perforated zinc at the top of each. Smartly they stripped up the cushions and unfastened from beneath each seat a canebottomed frame secreted there. In a moment, by opening certain ratchet holes in the wall of the carriage, they slid these in at a proper height above, and covered each with cushions and sleeping rug.

The Englishman went outside on the balcony, to be out of the way, and when he came back the whole place had been transformed. No longer an aisle of double seats, it was like a section of a proprietary chapel put snug for sleeping, with curtained berths and closed portholes.

'Oh, dexterous genius of Zenas Wallace and Ezra Jones, conductors of the New York Central Railway!' he recalled. The lights of the candle lamps were dimmed or withdrawn, and a hushed stillness pervaded the chambers of sleep. No sound broke it but the clump of the falling boots, and the button slapping sound of coats flung upon benches. Further on, within a second enclosure, one could hear voices of women and children.

A fat German haberdasher, from Cincinnati, was unrobing as if he were performing a religious ceremony, and, indeed, as the English gent noted, 'sleeping is a rehearsal of death, and seems rather a solemn thing, however we look at it.'

The bottom berths were singularly comfortable at first, with room to wander and explore, to roll and turn, and with curtains to hush all sound, and keep off all inquisitive rays from Zena's or Ezra's portable lamps. There was, indeed, twice the room that one would have had aboard an Atlantic steamer such as the one in which the Englishman would have come across. In a steamer berth, one could not sit up at night without bumping his or her head against the bed planks above, and could not turn without pulling one's bed covers off. As for a heavy sea, there was no keeping in bed at all without being lashed in.

'Now, I mount my berth; for sleep is sympathetic, and when everyone else goes to sleep I must, too,' said the Englishman. There were two berths to choose from, both of them just wicker trays, ledged in, cushioned and rugged, one about half a foot higher than the other.

'Several have turned in, and are snorting approval of themselves and of sleep as an institution generally,' he recalled of his fellow passengers. 'Others, like young crows, balancing on the spring boughs, swing their Yankee legs, lean and yellow, from the wicker trays, and peel off their stockings or struggle to get off their boots.

'I clambered to my perch. The tray was narrow and high. It was like lying with one's back on the narrow plank thrown across a torrent. If I turned my back to the carriage wall, the motion

Left: The Atlantic, a 'grasshopper' type locomotive, hauling the famous Inlay double-decked coaches. Built by Phineas Davis in 1832, this locomotive was in service for 60 years, a record in railroad history.

bumped me off my bed altogether; if I turned my face to the wall, I felt a horrible sensation of being likely to roll down backwards to be three minutes afterward picked up in detached portions. I lay on my back and so settled the question; but then the motion! The American railways are cheaply made and hastily constructed. They have often, on even great roads, but one line of rails, and that one line of rails is anything but even.

Through the night he heard the clashing of the bell on the engine at 'Chittenango,' 'Manlins,' 'Canton,' 'Jordon,' 'Canaserago' and all the other places with Indian, classical or scriptural names. When he peered through the zinc ventilator into outer darkness, a flying scud of sparks from the engine funnel did not serve to divest his mind of all chances of being burned. Then there were blazes of pine torches as they neared a station—a fresh bell clamor and jumbling sounds of baggage, slamming doors and itinerant conductors…

'I lay on my back on that wicker shelf of the sleeping car,' he continued, 'and in vain offered up prayers to the great black King Morpheus of the mandragora crown and ebon sceptre… No, zigzag goes the car, rush, jolts, and now I begin to believe the old story of the stoker and engineer playing cards all night, and now and then leaping the train over a "bad place," crying, "Go ahead; let her rip!"'

'At last a precarious and fragile sleep crusts me over, but it is like workhouse food; it keeps life together, but not amply or luxuriously. So blessed daylight reluctantly and sullenly returns, one by one we wake up, yawn and stretch ourselves. There is something suspicious in the haste with which we all flop out of bed; no really comfortable bed was ever left with such coarse ingratitude. Presently to us enter Zenas and Ezra, not to mention a new passenger from Crete, regardless of the somewhat effete atmosphere of our carriage, and proceed to adjust the seats.'

The beds would be rendered invisible in a few minutes. The wicker trays moved out and cushions stripped off, curtains put up to the roof supporters. Underpinning bolts—*Click*, *jolt*, and they were chair seats once more, and then through the open windows came a draught of pure air that freshens our frowzy and disheveled crew.

In the wash room, the one dirty scrub brush fastened to the wall by a chain gave the whole place the appearance of 'the cell of a dead barber.'

The Englishman was swift to mention that the *second* time he took a railroad sleeping car, he really *did* sleep, and the *third* time, he slept *well*.

'So much for habit,' he added.

Several hundred miles south of the New York Central's Hudson River Valley empire was that of the Baltimore & Ohio Railroad. From Philadelphia to Baltimore, the B&O passed along the top of Chesapeake Bay and then across the Susquehanna River. On one side of the river the cars were run onto a huge ferryboat, and again run off at the other side. Such an operation would seem to be one of difficulty under any circumstances; but the Susquehanna is a tidal river, rising and falling a considerable number of feet. The fathers of the B&O might have built a bridge, costing two or three million dollars, but in crossing the Susquehanna, the boat was so constructed that its deck was level with the line of the railroad at half tide, so that the inclined plane from the shore down to the boat, or from the shore up to the boat, never exceeded half the amount of the rise or fall.

As the British writer Anthony Trollope recalled, 'One would suppose that the most intricate machinery would have been necessary for such an arrangement; but it was all rough and simple, and apparently managed by two men. The cars were dragged up the inclined plane by a hawser attached to an engine,

which hawser, had the stress broken it, as I could not but fancy probable, would have flown back and cut to pieces a lot of us who were standing in front of the car. But I do not think that any such accident would have caused very much attention. Life and limbs are not held to be so precious here as they are in England.'

In his commentaries on American rail travel in the years immediately before the American Civil War, Trollope recalled another incident, on the Philadelphia & Reading Railroad, where in running down the mountains to Pittsburgh an accident occurred which 'in any other country would have thrown the engine off the line and reduced the carriages behind the engine to a heap of ruins. But here it had no other effect than that of delaying us for three or four hours. The tire of one of the heavy driving wheels flew off, and in the shock the body of the wheel itself was broken, one spoke and a portion of the circumference of the wheel carried were away, and the steam-chamber ripped open. Nevertheless, the train was pulled up, neither the engine nor any of the carriages got off the line, and the men in charge of the train seemed to think very lightly of the matter. I was amused to see how little of the affair was made by any of the passengers. In England a delay of three hours would in itself produce a great amount of grumbling, or at least many signs of discomfort and temporary unhappiness. But here no one said a word. Some of the younger men got out and looked at the ruined wheel; but most of the passengers kept their seats, chewed their tobacco, and went to sleep.'

A STRANGER IN A STRANGE LAND

An American traveling in England was in a first class railway compartment with two Englishmen. He lighted a cigar, and one of his companions said to him, 'I beg your pardon, but perhaps you have not noticed that there is a no smoking slip pasted on the window.'

'Oh, is there?' said the American, and kept on smoking.

Presently the Englishman said, 'Apparently you are not aware that in this country a fine is laid on persons who smoke in cars marked non-smoking.'

'Oh, is there?' said the American, and kept on smoking.

After a pause the Englishman, now angry, said, 'See here! We are coming to a station and I'm going to call the guard and have you put out.'

'Oh, are you?' said the American, and kept on smoking.

The train did stop presently and before the Englishman could do anything the American went to the door, let down the window and beckoned to the guard, 'Guard, there's a man in here,' pointing to the English spokesman, 'who is traveling first-class on a third-class ticket.'

'Will you please let me see your ticket?' said the guard to the Englishman, and, sure enough, his was a third-class ticket and he had to get out, hoist with his own petard.

The train went on. Presently the remaining Englishman said to the American, 'Pardon me, but I have a great curiosity to know how you knew that our neighbor was traveling on a third-class ticket.'

'That's easy,' said the American. 'His ticket was the same color as mine.'

—Rev Joseph Dunn Burrell

The fanciful 1949 advertisement *at right* poked fun at exactly the same kind of conditions experienced by the Englishman in the story on these pages. Electromotive was soon to become the world's largest maker of locomotives, but their locos would pull far fewer passengers than would have been predicted in 1949.

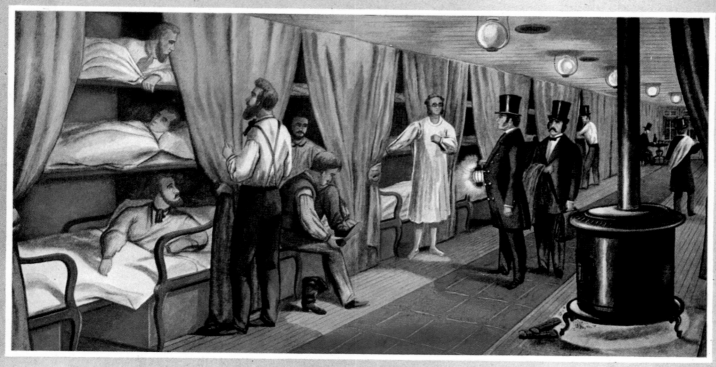

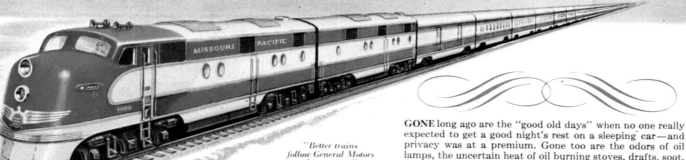

"Better trains
follow General Motors
Locomotives"

GONE long ago are the "good old days" when no one really expected to get a good night's rest on a sleeping car—and privacy was at a premium. Gone too are the odors of oil lamps, the uncertain heat of oil burning stoves, drafts, soot, cinders, and the jerky sleep-destroying stops and starts so familiar to old-time travelers.

★   ★   ★

HERE now are such fast, crack trains as the *Missouri Pacific Eagles* with luxurious private sleeping quarters that invite restful, unbroken slumber. Then, to make assurance of smooth, clean, on-time riding, these trains are powered by General Motors Diesel locomotives on their long journeys between St. Louis and Denver, and throughout the Southwest.

A roomy, sleep-inviting bedroom on a Missouri Pacific Eagle offers the comforts of a fine home, plus the ingenious planning of America's leading car builders.

Deep, refreshing sleep, free from jolts and jars and noise, is just one more proof that better trains follow General Motors locomotives. A good thing to remember when you plan your next trip—anywhere.

ELECTRO-MOTIVE DIVISION OF GENERAL MOTORS • LA GRANGE, ILL.

Home of the Diesel Locomotive

Above: East meets West as the last spike of the nation's first transcontinental railroad is driven home at Promontory, Utah on 10 May 1869. From the east came Union Pacific's *No 119* and vice president TC Durant, and from the west Central Pacific's *Jupiter*, pulling the private car of Leland Stanford. Stanford had actually arrived on 8 May and waited in the rain for two days. The rain stopped as the two locomotives paused within sight of one another, and the last rail was put in place.

Dignitaries from the nearby states gave speeches and presented Leland Stanford with gold, silver and iron spikes.

The gold spike was put into place and telegraph wires were attached to it, and to Stanford's hammer so that when the two came together, the moment would be heard simultaneously in both the East and the West. Stanford made a speech, and then a hush fell over the assembled crowd as Stanford of the Central Pacific swung a silver hammer at the gold spike. The hammer plunged

WHAT THE ENGINES SAID
(AT THE OPENING OF THE TRANSCONTINENTAL RAILROAD)

What was it the Engines said,
Pilots touching,—head to head
Facing on the single track,
Half a world behind each back?
This is chat the Engines said,
Unreported and unread.

With a prefatory screech,
In a florid Western speech,
Said the Engine from the West:
'I am from Sierra's crest;
And if altitude's a test,
Why, I reckon, it's confessed
That I've done my level best.'

Said the Engine from the East:
'They who work best talk the least.
S'pose you whistle down your brakes
What you've done is no great shakes,—
Pretty fair,—but let our meeting
Be a different kind of greeting.
Let these folks with champagne stuffing,
Not their Engines, do the *puffing*.'

'Listen! Where Atlantic beats
Shores of snow and summer heats;
Where the Indian autumn skies
Paint the woods with wampum dyes,—
I have chased the flying sun,
Seeing all he looked upon,
Blessing all that he has blessed,

Nursing in my iron breast
All his vivifying heat,
All his clouds about my crest;
And before my flying feet
Every shadow must retreat.'

Said the Western Engine, 'Phew!'
And a long, low whistle blew.
'Come, now, really that's the oddest
Talk for one so very modest.
You brag of your East! *You* do?
Why, *I* bring the East to *you*!
All the Orient, all Cathay,
Find through me the shortest way;
And the sun you follow here
Rises in my hemisphere.
Really,—if one must be rude,—
Length, my friend, ain't longitude.'

Said the Union: 'Don't reflect, or
I'll run over some Director.'
Said the Central 'I'm Pacific;
But, when riled, I'm quite terrific.
Yet today we shall not quarrel,
Just to show these folks this moral,
How two Engines—in their vision—
Once have met without collision.'
That is what the Engines said,
Unreported and unread;
Spoken slightly through the nose,
With a whistle at the close.

from *Complete Poetical Works*
by Bret Harte, 1898

downward toward the final notch in the steel belt that would bind the nation… and missed.

Stanford's second blow connected, but it was anticlimactic. Having seen the hammer fall, the telegraph technician, who was at his post waiting for this historic moment, had tapped his key to send the word across the country, and celebrations in Chicago and San Francisco had already begun.

As the cowcatchers of the two locomotives touched, the champagne flowed and the construction superintendents were photographed shaking hands. On the left is Samuel Montague of the Central Pacific and on the right is Grenville Dodge of the Union Pacific.

Note that the Central Pacific's *Jupiter* (left) has a huge, bell-shaped stack suitable for its wood-burning boiler, while the Union Pacific locomotive has a narrower stack indicative of its coal-fired boiler.

THE EXPERIENCE OF A NATION UNITED BY RAILS

Somewhere between the classic journey of Lewis and Clark and the first coast-to-coast flight of a commercial airliner, Americans experienced, then lost sight of and forgot, the first transcontinental trip of a railroad train pulled by a steam locomotive.

It was made in the summer of 1870, and it was more than a ten-day wonder. People, to be sure, had crossed the continent by rail before, but never via a through train. Few enough trains did thereafter, for that matter—until 1946, when a way to get through Chicago without changing trains was finally devised.

The daring travelers were members of the Boston Board of Trade, together with several of their wives and a few children. The group numbered 129, and was headed by Alexander H Rice, later governor of the Commonwealth of Massachusetts, containing family names of some potency in the professional, literary and mercantile circles of Boston—names like Brooks, Dana, Guild, Houghton, Kittredge, Longley, McIntire, Peabody and Warren. Notable publicity over a period of weeks had resulted in 50,000 people visiting the train during the two days it was on display in Boston.

On the day of departure a vast multitude was on hand at the depot to see the splendid procession of cars that had been built especially for this trip by George Pullman. They cheered mightily as the train pulled majestically out of the Boston & Albany station on the first leg of the long journey, while the locomotive engineer sounded his whistle in long, satisfying blasts, a practice he continued as far as Worcester.

It is fortunate that this Pullman Hotel Express party of 1870 included—as did the Lewis and Clark party of 1804—a competent observer who made note of all worthy things along the way and set them down for contemporaries and for posterity—not in this case in notebooks, but in all the authority of type and printer's ink. The observer was the journalist WR Steele, and in the baggage car of this extraordinary train was a 'brand new quarto-medium Gordon printing press,' on which—during the trip—he printed twelve issues of the first paper ever written, composed, printed and published on the rolling wheels of a steam railroad train. This paper was the *Trans-Continental*, now a rare piece of Americana indeed.

Editor Steele was patently aware of the importance of the event he was to chronicle. To impart the momentousness of this particular departure, he compared the '*All aboard*' of the train's conductor to the '*Yes*' spoken by Helen of Troy, to the 'nod of a Belgian peasant to Napoleon,' to the first trans-Atlantic cablegram—and went from there to liken the links binding the two American shores to the 'massive links in the Campo Santo at Pisa.'

Though we might compare it today to Neil Armstrong's 'small step for mankind,' classicism was not yet dead in Boston, and Boston was riding the rails.

There were eight elegant carriages to the train, reported Steele. The first in line was the baggage car, but such a baggage car was never before seen. It contained five ice closets and that shiny new quarto-medium Gordon printing press. Next came a handsome smoking car, in which was the editor's office, complete with black walnut cases for type, a smoking room with ochre tables, and a hair-dressing/shaving salon. Then came the two hotel cars, bearing names famous in the Bay State, the *Revere* and the *Arlington*. Of the two Palace Sleeping and Drawing Room cars, one was named *Palmyra*, with a slightly Mormon flavor, and *Marquette*. The commissary and dining cars were christened *St Cloud* and *St Charles*.

No one who saw it could fail to notice that the train was 'equipped with every desirable accessory tending to promote the ease of the passengers.' These accessories included elaborate hangings, costly upholstery, artistic gilding, and woodwork shining like a mirror. And, perhaps because it was a Boston party, there were two well-stocked libraries aboard—replete, said Editor Steele (a man of taste), with choice works of history, poetry and fiction.

To cap everything, there were two of the 'improved' Burdett organs. There must have been other music, too, for a roguish item in the first issue of the rolling newspaper said: 'Wanted—In the *Revere* Car, a Tenor and a Bass.' Apparently some of the Apleys were getting into voice.

At Albany, J Tillinghast, general superintendent of the New York Central, came aboard to ride as far as the suspension bridge at Niagara Falls, and was happy to see the Special do 304 miles in eight hours and 26 minutes. One spurt of 23 miles was done in 24 minutes.

Editor Steele took all this in stride, commenting on a subject that could have occurred to but few of his nineteenth century readers—that of time changes. Those of the party who kept their watches on Boston time, he pointed out rather smugly, would, upon arrival at San Francisco, find them three hours and 28 minutes too fast. He explained that in going West the time change was one minute for every 15 miles of longitude traversed. (The five North American Time Zones did not come into being until 18 November 1883.)

Although both the Boston & Albany and the New York

Above left: Steam locomotives arriving at Hornellville, as portrayed by Currier & Ives. *Above:* A poster proudly announces the grand opening of the Union Pacific Railroad. With the railroad's completion, a nation ravaged by a civil war was united, figuratively as well as literally. The West, though perceived as a vast, untamed wilderness, beckoned to those in the East, whether they came to start a new life or to experience a land unknown.

Central Railroads had shown every courtesy to the excursionists, it was the Michigan Central that really cut loose in 'fatted-calf' fashion. Picture the joy and amazement of the party when General Superintendent Sargent of that road had the *Ruby* rolled forward and hitched to the special. This locomotive was not only 'tastefully decorated with flowers,' but at her head was a large medallion which read 'Welcome to the Boston Board of Trade.' The tender was itself merely an easel for a 'panoramic landscape' of the trip from Boston to San Francisco, including views of the cities on the line.

Nor was that all. On either side of the elegant *Ruby*—between her drive wheels—the arms and shields of Massachusetts and California were painted in bright colors. To top everything, the *Ruby*'s great headlight was 'surmounted by a portrait of the President'—not of the *United States* of course, but of the *Michigan Central*!

Hospitality fairly deluged the special as it rolled westward. At Marshall, Michigan a huge tub of new butter was put aboard, compliments of Charles White, while at Detroit, KC Barker & Co presented the party with nothing less than two large boxes of superior fine-cut chewing tobacco—much to the comfort of the ruminant males.

At Chicago the Board of Trade and an immense concourse of people greeted the special. Speeches were made, and Chicago bade Godspeed to the party as it left over the Galena Division of the Chicago & Northwestern.

The party marveled at the steam-powered drawbridge over the mile-wide Mississippi and found Iowa a pleasant and prosperous land. Council Bluffs was discovered to be a rising city of 11,000, and the erudite editor told his readers that the place was named by Lewis and Clark, who 'held council' there with Indians.

Passengers heading west around the time of WR Steele's journey (see text) traveled in a car similar to the one *above*. The lucky ones, like Steele and his fellow travelers, enjoyed the comforts of a sleeping car *(above right)*. *Right*: Leland Stanford's private car.

Surprisingly enough—for the party was now really in the West—the amenities of civilization continued. A messenger boy was placed on board half an hour before meeting any eastbound mail, to collect letters for posting. At Omaha the public-spirited firm of Brewer & Bemis, knowing well the dryness of the Great Plains in summer, put aboard a barrel of their best ale, which was gratefully acknowledged by the editor. It was also at Omaha that the train turned to continue its westward journey on the tracks of the great Union Pacific—the railroad fathered by the dream of Abraham Lincoln!

Aesthetes were at large, too, even in these open spaces. At one of the stops, a 'very pleasant looking gentleman' appeared at a window and presented a young lady of the party with a bouquet. She thanked him, at which he 'lifted his hat and withdrew, bowing gracefully.' There was no end of surprises for the Bostonians.

It seems likely that the Omaha ale was beginning to work on Editor Steele, for between that city and Cheyenne he cut loose with a powerful editorial on 'The Age of Progress.' He also noticed that Columbus, population 800, was George Francis Train's geographical center of the United States, and that Train, a noted eccentric of the day, planned to move the national capital to Columbus when he was elected President.

Much of the scenery, particularly the endless flats of Nebraska and Wyoming, was not overly stimulating, yet the party remained of good cheer. Concerts on the two 'improved' Burdett organs were given, and voices 'rang forth with sweet and joyful notes.' They were singing and playing while thundering through the 'great night of the plains' at forty miles an hour.

Right: **This Currier & Ives print captures the beauty of a locomotive rolling through the Tennessee countryside.** *Above:* **The richly upholstered chairs on this parlor car built by the Pullman Palace Car Company revolved on swivels allowing the passenger to turn and gaze at the incredible scenery just outside the window.**

The excursionists had been avid for a sight of the herds of bison, but they saw mere small groups of this animal along the North Fork of the Platte. Gophers, however, were everywhere, and of course Editor Steele was ready for them.

'The gopher,' he remarked, scarcely able to contain himself, 'is so called because he will "go fer" the farmer's grain.'

Passing through the Wasatch Range of the Rockies, north of Salt Lake City, called forth general excitement, and some fine lyrical periods in the paper. These sights were viewed from an observation car, which the courteous men of the Central Pacific Railroad had attached to the train.

The tracks of the Union Pacific Railroad joined those of the Central Pacific at Ogden, just north of the Great Salt Lake. The Central Pacific, headquartered in San Francisco and presided over by Leland Stanford, was noted for its grand flamboyance.

This mood was, of course, in stark contrast to the lifestyle of the Mormons of the Salt Lake City region. Nevertheless, the Mormons knew how to make the desert bloom and how to organize a country. Even the Bostonians, perhaps as well informed a group of gentiles as could be found in the East, were astonished at the great work accomplished in a short time. By invitation of George Pullman himself, a delegation of Mormon leaders dined on board the train, which included President Brigham Young, Senator Wilfred Woodruff, George Cannon and Brigham Young, Jr.

One wonders if the Bostonians realized what a personage they dined with that day in Salt Lake City. Did they consider Young merely as a freak or a shrewd, if eccentric, opportunist? Or did they consider him to be a man of genuine stature, of accomplishments as impressive as any of his time?

At any rate, they found him gregarious—and informative, too. He told his hosts that he then had 16 wives and 49 living children—an announcement that was probably received with mixed emotions. He further reported that he was 69 years of age, and had attended school but 11 days in all his life.

President Young also invited the party to the Mormon Tabernacle. There, if not before, Boston was more than impressed—by the size and the magnificence of the building—but even more so by the 'remarkable address' of Mr Young, which he delivered with an ease and sureness not often encountered.

Filled with a new respect for the abilities of Mormons, the Pullman Hotel Express pulled away for the long haul to the Pacific, while talk turned to the wonders of transportation and communication. Out here in the region of vast spaces, where Boston seemed so far away, the magic of the telegraph was brought home. One of the party had sent a wire home to learn if his family was well, and 'we had scarce run 47 miles further when the reply was received.'

It all set Editor Steele to pondering that this wonderful communications medium should be so strong a channel between the train and friends at home that it could transmit 'intelligence' in the twinkling of an eye. Perhaps, he brooded in print, the same or a similar principle might be expanded and applied to locomotion, annihilating distance and almost outrunning time.

The special pounded on, through Hot Springs, Willard City, and Corinne, and then past Promontory, where the golden spike had been pounded only a year before—linking the Union Pacific to the Central Pacific, the eastern United States to the golden west of California.

Human desert rats, even then wandering the high, dry places of the land, paused a moment in their endless search for the

Right: Daring Sante Fe passengers climb down the mountainous terrain of the Wild West to be photographed and thus to preserve the memory of their exciting trip through Indian country.

mountains of silver and the ledges of gold to watch the Pullman Hotel Express following the example of Lewis and Clark, looking with what seemed to be either mild interest or mild disgust at the gaudy cars.

At last the train made its way over the Sierra at Summit, then down through the American River Canyon to Sacramento, and finally to the glittering jewel — San Francisco. The barrel of Omaha ale must have long since evaporated. Then, a bottle of another beverage — Massachusetts Bay water — was emptied into San Francisco Bay, with all of the amenities proper to such an occasion.

The Boston Board of Trade party was taken in hand by masters of showmanship. The Bostonians were wined, dined, praised, taken for trips to the Mother Lode and through Yosemite Valley.

On 25 June 1870, punctual to the minute, 'our beloved train, which had been tastefully decorated' left Oakland on the return trip. They saw Indians this time, and ran into vast swarms of locusts that often impeded their progress by making the tracks so slippery that the wheels spun without providing forward motion.

At Omaha the irrepressible George Francis Train showed up to greet the party and to tell them he was about to start his trip around the world, which he hoped to make in no more than 90 days. At Council Bluffs the Bostonians had a message from — though they did not meet — Mrs Amelia Bloomer, former editor of *The Lily*, a temperance paper, and designer of a garment that had already taken her name.

At half-past six, on 2 July 1870, six weeks to the day from its departure, the Pullman Hotel Express pulled back into Boston. The trip had been a tremendous experience for all. They were wiser people for their journey, certainly better Americans. Editor Steele, on the whole an alert and competent reporter, and a reflective man as well, summed up when he arrived back at Tremont Street.

'Thank God!' he cried, 'that we have a Massachusetts, a Maine, and a California, and for all the noble Commonwealths of the sisterhood of states... It shall not be our fault if the glorious promise of the future in fame and progress be not fulfilled.'

That was it. The Union, the glorious Union, and she was now flying with her own wings, flying high and handsome, Destiny in her talons.

The men and women of Boston had now seen Cheyenne

Above: **The Pullman Company even built barber shop cars!** *Right:* **A nostalgic Currier & Ives depiction of a train trapped by a snow storm.**

Below: Not everything was golden in passenger railroading's golden era. Take, for example, this collapse of a trestle at Lake Labish in Oregon on 12 November 1890.

Indians in their own habitat. They had seen and talked with Mormons, prospectors, cowhands, homesteaders and farmers of the West. They'd met lumberjacks and trappers. They had seen the great fertile acres of the Midwest, the illimitable grasslands, the deserts, the strange rock formations of Wyoming, the mighty cliffs of the Rockies and the Sierra, the wild blue of the Pacific. It was all America, all the United States, warp and woof, good and bad. This was the mood of America at the time, and it was the railroads that had made it possible for Americans to manifest this mood.

The men and women of the Boston Board of Trade would never be quite the same again. They had seen a California Redwood tree that was immeasurably bigger and taller than the column in Mr Breed's pasture in Charlestown. They had crossed rivers that made the Charles seem like the drippings of an eave's spout. More important, they had seen at first hand how many miles stretched across America, and how those miles had been caught and tamed by the rails and the wires—not only *caught and tamed*, but *bound together*. Henceforth, the words 'United States of America' would mean something new, something infinitely greater.

In 1873—four years after the completion of the first transcontinental rail line and three years after the odyssey of the Pullman Hotel Express—a plucky English spinster named Isabella Lucy Bird decided to explore the scenic wonders of the Colorado Rockies, a feat which she accomplished largely on horseback and packing a pistol. Her rail trip, her many adventures on the raw frontier and the unusual characters she encountered there were described in letters she sent home to her sister Henrietta.

'It is a weariness to go back,' she wrote, 'even in thought, to the clang of San Francisco, which I left in its cold morning fog early yesterday, driving to the Oakland ferry through streets

Above: Coach cars, circa 1865, were lit by oil lamps. Jennie Stanford—the daughter of Leland Stanford, president of both the Southern Pacific and the Central Pacific—received complimentary passes *(below)* every year. *Facing page, above:* An annual pass issued by the Central Pacific. *Facing page, below:* The Southern Pacific Passenger Station in San Francisco prior to the devastating earthquake of 1906.

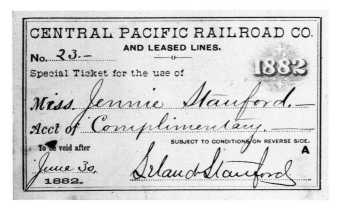

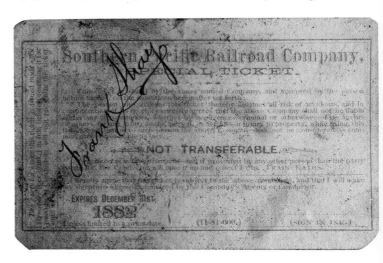

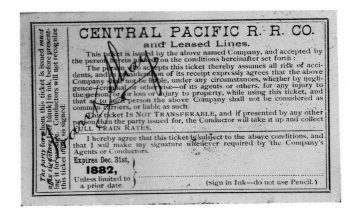

with sidewalks heaped with thousands of cantaloupes and watermelons, tomatoes, cucumbers, squashes, pears, grapes, peaches, apricots—all of startling size as compared with any I ever saw before. Other streets were piled with sacks of flour, left out all night, owing to the security from rain at this summer season.

'In the late afternoon (of the following day), we began the ascent of the Sierras (on the Central Pacific line), whose sawlike points had been in sight for many miles. The dusty fertility was all left behind, and the country became rocky, gravelly and deeply scored by streams bearing the muddy wash of the mountain gold mines down to the muddier Sacramento. There were long, broken ridges and deep ravines, the ridges becoming longer, the ravines deeper, the pines thicker and larger, as we ascended into a cool atmosphere of exquisite purity, and before six pm the last traces of cultivation and the last hardwood trees were left behind.

'At Colfax, a Central Pacific Railway station at a height of 2400 feet, I got out and walked the length of the train. First came two great, gaudy engines, the *Grizzly Bear* and the *White Fox*, with their respective tenders loaded with logs of wood, the engines with great, solitary reflecting lamps in front above the cow guards, a quantity of polished brasswork, comfortable glass houses, and well-stuffed seats for the engine-drivers. The engines and tenders were succeeded by a baggage car, the latter loaded with bullion and valuable parcels, and in charge of two 'express agents.' Each of these cars is 45 feet long. Then came two cars loaded with peaches and grapes; then two 'Silver Palace' cars, each 60 feet long; then a smoking car, at that time occupied mainly by Chinamen; and then five ordinary passenger cars, with platforms like all the others, making altogether a train about 700 feet in length.

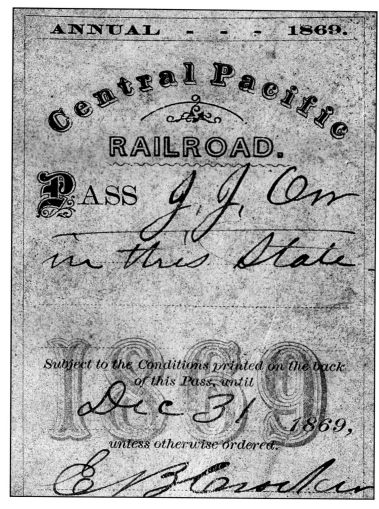

'Shivering in the keen, frosty air near the summit pass of the Sierras, we entered the "snow-sheds"—wooden galleries which, for about 50 miles, shut out all the splendid views of the region, as given in dioramas—not even allowing a glimpse of 'the Gem of the Sierras,' the lovely Donner Lake. One of these sheds is 27 miles long. In a few hours, the mercury had fallen from 103 degrees (at Sacramento) to 19 degrees, and we had ascended 6987 feet in 105 miles! After passing through the sheds, we had several grand views of a pine forest on fire before reaching Truckee at 11 pm, having traveled 258 miles.

'Precisely at 11 pm, the huge Pacific train, with its heavy bell tolling, thundered up to the door of the Truckee House, and on presenting my ticket at the double door of a 'Silver Palace' car, the slippered steward, whispering low, conducted me to my berth—a luxurious bed three and a half feet wide, with a hair mattress on springs, fine linen sheets and costly California blankets. The 24 inmates of the car were all invisible, asleep behind rich curtains. It was a true Temple of Morpheus. Profound sleep was the object to which everything was dedicated. Four silver lamps hanging from the roof, and burning low, gave a dreamy light. On each side of the center passage, rich red curtains, green and crimson, striped with gold, hung from silver bars running near the roof, and trailed on the soft Axminster carpet. The temperature was carefully kept at 70 degrees, while it was 29 degrees outside. Silence and freedom from jolting were secured by double doors and windows, comely and ingenious arrangements of springs and cushions, and a speed limited to 18 miles an hour.

'As I lay down, the gallop under the dark pines, the frosty moon, the forest fires, the flaring lights and roaring din of Truckee faded as dreams fade, and eight hours later a pure, pink dawn divulged a level, blasted region, with grey sagebrush growing out of a soil encrusted with alkali, and bounded on either side by low, glaring ridges. All through that day we traveled under a cloudless sky over solitary, glaring plains, and stopped twice at solitary, glaring frame houses, where coarse, greasy meals, infested by lazy flies, were provided at a dollar per head. By evening we were running across the continent on a bee line, and I sat for an hour on the rear platform of the rear car to enjoy the wonderful beauty of the sunset and the atmosphere. As far as one could see in the crystalline air there was nothing but desert. The jagged Humboldt ranges flaming in the sunset, with snow in their clefts, though 45 miles off, looked within an easy

canter. The bright metal track, purpling like all else in the cool distance, was all that linked one with Eastern or Western civilization.

'The next morning, when the steward unceremoniously turned us out of our berths soon after sunrise, we were running down upon the Great Salt Lake, bounded by the white Wasatch range. At the Mormon town of Ogden we changed cars, and again traversed dusty plains, white and glaring, varied by muddy streams and rough, arid valleys, now and then narrowing into canyons. By common consent, the windows were kept closed to exclude the fine white alkaline dust, which is very irritating to the nostrils. The journey became more and more wearisome as we ascended rapidly over immense plains and wastes of gravel destitute of mountain boundaries, and with only here and there a 'knoll' or 'butte' to break the monotony. The wheel-marks of the trail to Utah often ran parallel with the track, and bones of oxen were bleaching in the sun, the remains of those 'whose carcasses fell in the wilderness' on the long, dry journey. The daybreak of today (Sunday) found us shivering at Fort Laramie, Wyoming, a frontier post dismally situated at a height of 7000 feet. Another 1000 feet over gravelly levels brought us to Sherman, the highest level reached by this (Union Pacific) railroad. From this point eastward the streams fall into the Atlantic. The ascent of these apparently level plateaus is called 'crossing the Rocky Mountains,' but I have seen nothing of the range, except two peaks like teeth lying low on the distant horizon. It became mercilessly cold; some people thought it snowed, but I saw only rolling billows of fog. Lads passed through the cars the whole morning, selling newspapers, novels, lollipops, popcorn, peanuts, and ivory ornaments, so that, having lost all reckoning of the days, I never knew that it was Sunday till the cars pulled up at the door of the hotel in this detestable place (Cheyenne).

'Below the hotel window, freight cars are being perpetually shunted, but beyond the railroad tracks are nothing but the brown plains, with their lonely sights—now a solitary horseman at a traveling amble, then a party of Indians in paint and feathers, but civilized up to the point of carrying firearms.'

Below, left to right: A Southern Pacific employee season ticket, an SP ticket and the first official time schedule for the Central Pacific. *At right:* Assorted tickets and transfers for western railroads, circa 1898. Note the ticket for 'Deck Passage for One Chinaman' (bottom left) issued by the Oregon Steam Navigation Company. Numerous Chinese immigrants helped to build America's western railroads.

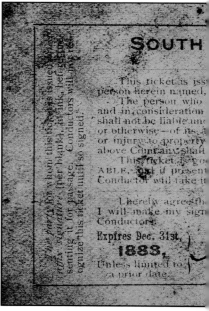

PORTLAND
TO
ASHLAND.
Not good unless dated on back and used
within thirty (30) days from date of sale.
Liability for baggage limited to $100.
H. Goodman
GEN. PASS. AND TICKET AGENT

OREGON & CALIFORNIA R. R. Co
TRANSFER TICKET
5 CENTS.
Geo. Rogers
Gen'l Pass Agt.

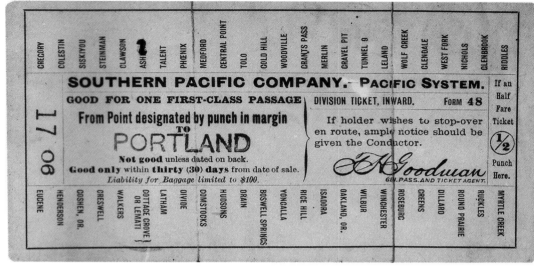

SOUTHERN PACIFIC COMPANY. PACIFIC SYSTEM.

GOOD FOR ONE FIRST-CLASS PASSAGE

From Point designated by punch in margin
TO
PORTLAND

Not good unless dated on back.
Good only within thirty (30) days from date of sale.
Liability for Baggage limited to $100.

DIVISION TICKET, INWARD.   FORM 48

If holder wishes to stop-over
en route, ample notice should be
given the Conductor.

H. Goodman
GEN. PASS. AND TICKET AGENT.

If an
Half
Fare
Ticket
1/2
Punch
Here.

Stations listed (top margin): GREGORY, COLESTIN, SISKIYOU, STEINMAN, CLAWSON, ASH, TALENT, PHENIX, MEDFORD, CENTRAL POINT, TOLO, GOLD HILL, WOODVILLE, GRANT'S PASS, MERLIN, GRAVEL PIT, TUNNEL 9, LELAND, WOLF CREEK, GLENDALE, WEST FORK, NICHOLS, GLENBROOK, RIDDLES

Stations listed (bottom margin): EUGENE, HENDERSON, GOSHEN, OR., CRESWELL, WALKERS, COTTAGE GROVE OR LEMATI, LATHAM, DIVIDE, COMSTOCKS, HUDSONS, DRAIN, BOSWELL SPRINGS, YONCALLA, RICE HILL, ISADORA, OAKLAND, OR., WILBUR, WINCHESTER, ROSEBURG, GREENS, DILLARD, ROUND PRAIRIE, RUCKLES, MYRTLE CREEK

Portland & Willamette Valley Railway Co.
Good for One First-Class Passage.
OSWEGO TO PORTLAND.
640
William Reid
Vice President.
FORM R. E.

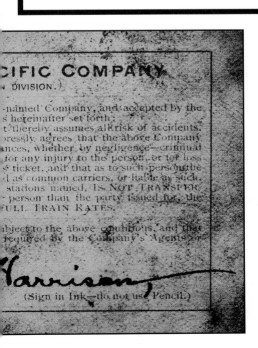

Oregon Steam Navigation Co.
368

DECK PASSAGE.

PORTLAND to KALAMA.

ONE CHINAMAN.

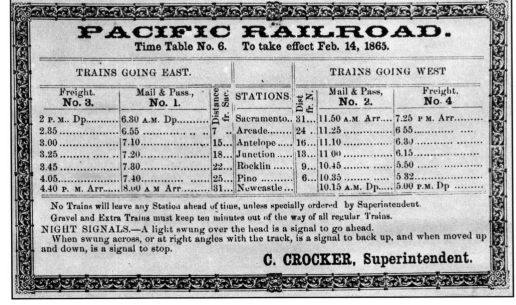

OREGON RAILWAY NAVIGATION CO.
LOCAL TICKET.
ONE FIRST CLASS PASSAGE
C
To
No 47
John Muir
Gen'l Passenger Agent.

...CIFIC COMPANY
... DIVISION.)

...named Company, and accepted by the
...s hereinafter set forth.
...t thereby assumes all risk of accidents.
...ressly agrees that the above Company
...ances, whether by negligence—criminal
...for any injury to the person, or to loss
...s ticket, and that as to such persons he
...d as common carriers, or liable as such
...stations named, IS NOT TRANSFER...
...person than the party issued for, the
...FULL TRAIN RATES.
...bject to the above conditions, and that
...required by the Company's Agents...

Harrison
(Sign in Ink—do not use Pencil.)

PACIFIC RAILROAD.
Time Table No. 6.   To take effect Feb. 14, 1865.

Freight. No. 3.	Mail & Pass., No. 1.	Distance fr. Sac.	STATIONS.	Dist. fr. N.	Mail & Pass, No. 2.	Freight. No. 4.
2 P.M. Dp.........	6.30 A.M. Dp.........		Sacramento.	31	11.50 A.M. Arr......	7.25 P.M. Arr.........
2.35	6.55	7	Arcade........	24	11.25	6 55 ....
3.00	7.10	15	Antelope	16	11.10	6.30 ....
3.25	7.20	18	Junction	13	11 00	6.15 ....
3.45	7.30	22	Rocklin	9	10.45	5.50 ....
4.05	7.40	25	Pino	6	10.35	5 32 ....
4.40 P.M. Arr	8.00 A.M Arr	31	Newcastle ...		10.15 A.M. Dp	5.00 P.M. Dp ....

No Trains will leave any Station ahead of time, unless specially ordered by Superintendent.
Gravel and Extra Trains must keep ten minutes out of the way of all regular Trains.
NIGHT SIGNALS.—A light swung over the head is a signal to go ahead.
When swung across, or at right angles with the track, is a signal to back up, and when moved up
and down, is a signal to stop.

C. CROCKER, Superintendent.

THE PULLMAN THAT GOT AWAY

Tom Burnley is a man most of us have never heard about. Yet his name is mentioned in the same breath with those individuals who refused to back Henry Ford in his early days—with those foolish few who could have bought, at the birth of Coca-Cola, a half-interest in the company for a pittance but thought it too long a shot to risk.

It happened back in 1860 in Canada. The Prince of Wales (who later was to become King Edward VII of England) was scheduled to make a tour of the Canadian provinces. Looking over the Prince's itinerary, the Governor General of Canada immediately saw that there would be much overnight travel between cities, a situation that would involve finding some sort of sleeping arrangements for the crown prince. He advertised for bids for the construction of a railroad coach which would be used, besides ordinary travel, for sleeping quarters for the distinguished visitor while enroute.

Among the designs submitted for the unheard-of contraption were those of Tom Burnley. His plans were chosen and he got the government go ahead. His coach, an elaborate creation, was built in the Brantford, Ontario railyards under the supervision of Burnley himself. This coach boasted hand-carved, gilded coats of arms on each side, marble wash basins and counters, finely paneled walls, overstuffed beds, couches and chairs, and heavy, tassel-fringed draperies.

When the Prince finally arrived and saw his new home on wheels, he was delighted with it. He used it in preference to hotels, and it was his official address for the two months of his tour.

Poor Tom Burnley could not see the future of such a monstrosity and blindly forgot to patent his coach. It was beyond the realm of his imagination that such a sleeping coach could be put into widespread use. After all, he thought, who would want to sleep on a train?

But at that same time, there was also another unknown, who was coming to Brantford on occasional trips. His name was George Pullman (*see page 62*) and he was employed by the Buffalo & Lake Erie Railway. Having occasion to visit the yards at Brantford, he heard about the strange railway coach that was being built, and out of curiosity went to have a look.

Being no idle dreamer, he realized the possibilities of the sleeping coach, and after making careful sketches and asking many pointed questions, he returned to Buffalo and secretly began to construct a coach of his own. Duly constructed and patented, the coach was put into use on the railway. It was an immediate success, and by using shrewd business acumen in renting the cars rather than selling them, Pullman was on his way to becoming a millionaire.

So Tom Burnley's invention, evolving from a gaudy Victorian sleeping coach designed for a king, became a blessing to weary travelers. But Tom Burnley himself has long been forgotten—hidden in the musty archives of inventors and inventions—remembered by a scanty few as an inventor who might had made a million if…

—*Thomas P Ramirez*

At right: A club car, circa 1900, appointed with comfortable leather chairs, writing tables and even spittoons.

THE FRED HARVEY STORY

By Pamela Berkman

Frederick Henry Harvey has often been credited with civilizing the West. Certainly he brought gastronomic delights and hospitality beyond many cattlemen's wildest dreams to a business sorely in need of them.

Before Harvey made his mark, food along the rails was notorious. Dining cars had not yet made their appearance, so meals were served at railroad depots. Trains had to stop at mealtimes, usually for only 10 minutes. Passengers paid about 50 cents in advance for a lunch or supper of rancid bacon, canned beans, eggs, bitter coffee and 'sinkers'—heavy biscuits.

To top it all off, these roadhouses were often in league with the train crews. Almost as soon as the customers were served, the train whistle blew, the conductor called 'All aboard!' and the passengers had to make a run for the train, leaving most of the meal uneaten. The beanery served what was left to the next victim, and paid off the train crew at a dime a passenger.

Enter Fred Harvey, a low-key, gentlemanly Englishman with exquisite taste and an appreciation for good food and pleasant surroundings. Under his guidance, the Atchinson, Topeka and Santa Fe Railroad gained a reputation for fine dining and hospitality unsurpassed by any American railroad before or since.

Harvey was born in London in 1835, the son of a Scottish-English couple. At the age of 15, Harvey left England with two pounds sterling and a ticket to New York in his pocket. A few days after arriving, he got a job as a 'pot whalloper' at the Smith & McNeill restaurant and bar at 229 Washington Street.

Somehow, he managed to save a few dollars from his meager salary, and once again used his savings for passage, this time to New Orleans. After a bout with yellow fever, he found another restaurant job, and then used the savings from it to buy a ticket to St Louis.

By now it was 1853, and St Louis—the 'Gateway to the West'—was a bustling, vibrant city of 150,000. Waterfront warehouses, smoking factories and riverboat paddle wheelers provided the backdrop for the realization of young Fred Harvey's dream—to open his own restaurant. By 1859 he had found a partner and opened a successful eating place. In 1860 he married 18-year-old Barbara Sarah 'Sally' Mattas, a beautiful Bohemian girl born in Prague.

But this happy and prosperous time was not to last. with the outbreak of the Civil War in 1861, Harvey's business partner, who, unlike Harvey, sympathized with the South, absconded with all the restaurant funds, leaving the young entrepreneur with no business and no money.

Harvey then went to work for the Mississippi River Packet Line, owned by Captain Rufus Ford, which ran to St Joseph. In 1862 Harvey was hired as a distributing clerk in the St Joseph mailroom, and then as a postal worker on the mail cars on the Hannibal & St Joseph Railroad—a pioneering Western railroad known more widely as the 'Horrible and Slow Jolting.' This was Harvey's introduction to the deplorable state of railroad food and accommodations, and the beginning of his long association with the rails.

By 1865 Harvey had risen in the railroad business to become the general western agent for the North Missouri Railroad and was transferred to Leavenworth, Kansas, where he eventually purchased a home. The house is still a Leavenworth showplace, and is now on the National Register of Historic Places. Built by AA Higginbotham in 1875 and sold to Harvey for $24,856, the three-story building is made of sawn and handcarved limestone; lacy detailing adorns the roof and the front entrance.

With his new-found prosperity, Harvey got into the restaurant business again. He and a partner, Jeff Rice, opened two eating establishments, one each in the Kansas towns of Hugo and Wallace. After a few months, the two men parted company, dividing up the profits. Harvey then went to the Burlington Railroad with an idea to provide quality food and service to travelers through cooperation between the railroad and himself. The Burlington wasn't interested.

Harvey then approached Charles Morse, superintendent of the Santa Fe Railroad, whom he had known as a co-worker during his brief stint at the Burlington. Morse also appreciated fine dining and thought that Harvey's ideas had possibilities. They persuaded WS Strong, Santa Fe's general manager at the time, to give it a try. Thus it was that the first of many 'Harvey Houses' was opened—in Topeka, Kansas.

Harvey purchased a small restaurant in the old Topeka depot and office building. He closed it down for two days, scrubbed it thoroughly, bought high quality tablecloths and napkins, polished the silver, and stocked up on better food. The Santa Fe provided the space and some materials and supplies on a handshake deal, which, for a very long time, was the only kind of deal Harvey made with the Santa Fe. He believed that when gentlemen did business, no other guarantee was needed.

Within a few weeks the Topeka eating house was doing a capacity business. The Santa Fe agreed that Harvey's experiment had been a success. They expanded the operation in 1877 by purchasing a run down hotel on the line at Florence. Harvey, his wife and his sister picked out mattresses, cooking equipment and heavy walnut furniture. Harvey ordered Sheffield silver from England and fine table linens from Ireland. The glassware was first-rate. The chef was hired away from Chicago's famed Palmer House Hotel for $5000 a year, making him easily the wealthiest man in Florence.

Florence was awed. A tiny hamlet of about 100 people with no inherent importance except the fact that it was on a railroad, it had never seen the likes of this Harvey House. Farmers prospered. The Chicago chef paid top prices for prairie chickens, quail and fresh butter, fruits and vegetables.

Word of mouth made the Florence House food and accommodations famous. Soon travelers were flocking to the Santa Fe because it was the only railroad that provided passengers with

Fred Harvey (*above*) revolutionized food service on railroads by turning quick and greasy meal stops into a pleasant dining experience. The waitresses were young, pretty and pleasant; the tables were set with fine linens and silver; and the food was always fresh and perfectly prepared. Though the restaurants often lost money, they were an asset for Sante Fe because they drew passengers to their routes.

were talking about it, and more business was coming its way than it could handle, there was the usual opportunity to cash in on the good reputation to shade down service and shade up prices.

'My father was very well aware of this opportunity of course, but he also saw in the situation a peculiar opportunity to build good will. People would be expecting him to let down a little in his care for their interests under all this prosperity. And he saw that if he did not let down then, they would notice it and appreciate it all the more; they would feel all the more that they could rely on his service. And again he did not let down.'

Temptations to let customers down abounded, but Harvey gave in to none of them. There was, for instance, the milk problem in Arizona. Getting the necessary supplies to the restaurants was difficult during the early days of expansion in the Southwest. In those days, milk could not be brought into Arizona from the dairy country because the distance was too great and it would have spoiled; furthermore, it could not be bought in the state, as there were not sufficient milk-producing herds.

Harvey did not have to supply milk. If he had not, he would not have suffered by comparison with other Arizona eateries. None of them had it. Customers would have understood that fresh milk was unobtainable in the deserts of Arizona. But Harvey established his own dairy farm there to supply his Arizona Houses. And when he had trouble because the right kind of cows could not be bought there and did not do well when they were shipped in, he established his own nursery for the cattle.

Even during the Depression no skimping was allowed in a Harvey establishment. During one inspection it was revealed that a manager had stretched his meat supply to provide 156 steaks. He received a stern reprimand from his supervisor and was told that he should have gotten only 141 steaks from his supply.

Harvey insisted on keeping the quality of the food and service high and the cost to customers low. Meals cost 50 cents at first, then stayed at 75 cents until 1918, when they went up to one dollar. At lunch counters, where the price was even lower, the quality was as high but there was less of a variety of food.

A typical 75 cent Harvey dinner menu in 1888 offered diners a diversity, including blue points on shell, English peas au gratin, filet of whitefish in madeira sauce, potatoes francaise, young capon with hollandaise sauce, roast sirloin of beef au jus, pork with applesauce, stuffed turkey with cranberry sauce, mashed potatoes, sweet potatoes, Elgin sugar corn, marrowfat peas, asparagus in cream sauce, salami of duck, queen olives, baked veal pie, charlotte of peaches with cognac sauce, prairie chicken with currant jelly, sugar cured ham, pickled lamb's tongue, lobster salad, beets, celery and French slaw. This does not include the dessert offerings of different fruits, ice cream, cakes, specialties such as cold custard a la chantilly and catawba wine jelly, and cheeses with water crackers and coffee. Customers were in theory welcome to partake of all of these dishes, although in practice they usually limited their choices to a few.

The surroundings the meals were served in were no less impressive. After things got rolling, most of the Harvey Houses, especially those in the Southwest, were designed by architect Mary Colter. Colter had a keen sense of the Indian and Spanish heritage of the region, and planned the buildings with this in mind. At her suggestion, Native American motifs were used on walls, menus and even specially created china. Thus, from the foundations of the hotels to the smallest detail on the table, Harvey Houses blended beautifully with the landscape and the mood of the Southwest.

decent meals. The success of the Harvey Houses was measured in this way—by the passengers they brought to the Santa Fe; they were not expected to make large profits in and of themselves. Frequently they did not, and even lost money.

One Harvey House, for instance, consistently lost $1000 per month. When a new manager was hired, he sliced this loss to $500 a month by serving smaller portions and lower quality food. He proudly boasted of his achievement, until word of it reached Fred Harvey's ears. Harvey fired the manager, although he eventually cooled off and placed him at another hotel. The Harvey House, to Mr Harvey's pleasure, went back to serving good food and losing $1000 a month.

As one of Harvey's sons explained in a 1921 article:

'Of course the opportunity to increase immediate profits by letting down on service grew as the business established itself. After the Florence Hotel got underway, for example, and people

Fine fare and dining rooms such as Harvey offered would alone have assured a solid reputation and return customers among both the train travelers and the locals, with whom the Houses were equally popular. But as if these things weren't enough, Harvey introduced the 'Harvey Girls,' and went on to win the West as no lawman could have done.

Harvey wanted standards of service as high as his standards of cuisine. He placed ads in Eastern and Midwestern newspapers: 'Wanted: Young women of good character, attractive and intelligent, 18 to 30.' Experience was not essential, but good character was. Under the stern, watchful eye of a veteran Harvey matron, girls were in by 10 o'clock, slept in dormitories, and did their hair plainly but prettily (no fancy hairdos allowed), always tied in back with a simple white ribbon. Their uniforms of black dress, black stockings and black shoes had to be neatly cleaned and pressed at all times. They dished up welcome and good cheer, as well as meals, to customers. Wrote SE Kiser:
'Oh, the pretty Harvey Girl beside my chair
   A fairer maiden I shall never see
She was winsome, she was neat, she was gloriously sweet,
   And she certainly was very good to me.'

JC Davis of Devore, California had this to say: 'Harvey Houses, don't you savvy? clean across the old Mojave. On the Santa Fe they've strung 'em like a string of Indian beads. We all couldn't eat without 'em, but the slickest thing about 'em, is the Harvey skirts that hustle up the feeds.'

Writer Elbert Hubbard, reviewing Santa Fe service for his publication *The Fra* in 1909, wrote: 'At Fred Harvey's you are always expected. The girls are ever in their best bib and tucker, spotlessly gowned, manicured, combed, dental flossed— bright, healthy, intelligent girls—girls that are never fly, flip nor fresh, but who give you the attention that never obtrudes, but which is hearty and heartfelt.

'You note the immaculate linen, the shining silver, the dainty fruits and flowers, and your heart is full of admiration for Fred Harvey, great and good, shy and modest, industrious and persistent, restless and brave, who set the world such a pace in catering that the effete and dreamy East can only imitate it.

When their waitressing careers were behind them, many a Harvey Girl would stay in the West and make some lucky rancher or farmer a wonderful wife. Harvey Girls *(above)* in Hutchinson, Kansas take a brief break on a sunny afternoon in 1915. *Right:* The Harvey House and Santa Fe Station in Amarillo, Texas.

'I have it on the reliable authority of Mendelssohn himself, tourist agent, that a Fred Harvey Girl lasts on the desert only about six months, when she forfeits her pay, marries a millionaire mine owner or ranchman, and they settle down and are happy ever afterward. The first born boy is always and forever named Fred Harvey.'

It is said that Fred Harvey furnished the West with good food and fine wives. Despite the generous salary—$17.50 per month, room, board and tips (and Harvey Girls were usually tipped, and tipped well)—many girls did marry soon after beginning their employment. They had to promise verbally when signing up not to marry for a year. Harvey, however, accepted philosophically the fact that girls 'of good character, attractive and intelligent' wouldn't last long on the prairies and in the desert without being snatched up. He would frequently stage parties for the newlyweds. But he also congratulated any girl who got through her first six months without an engagement ring. Experience showed that if a Harvey Girl could hold out that long, she usually stayed unmarried for another three or four years.

For the most part, the girls—with their demure decorum and poise—married quite well, either becoming brides of Santa Fe engineers, conductors and station agents, or well-to-do Western ranchers and farmers. The grand total of Harvey Girls who became Western wives has been estimated at 5000. There is also a legend, far from proved, that more than 4000 babies were christened 'Fred' or 'Harvey'—or both—after these marriages.

The girls even inspired the 1946 movie *The Harvey Girls*, which starred Judy Garland. It is this film that is the source of the famous song extolling the virtues of 'The Atchison, Topeka and Santa Fe.'

THE HARVEY GIRL

I have seen some splendid paintings in my day
And I have looked at faultless statuary;
I've seen the orchard trees abloom in May
And watched their colors in the shadows vary;
I have viewed the noblest shrines in Italy
And gazed upon the richest mosques of Turkey,
But the fairest of all sights, it seems to me,
Was a Harvey Girl I saw in Albuquerque.

O that pretty Harvey Girl was good to see,
Her presence and her manner made me glad;
As she heaped things on my plate,
I kept busy thanking Fate
For her deftness and the appetite I had.

I have heard the wind blow softly through the trees,
I have listed to the robin blithely singing;
I have heard the mellow sounds float on the breeze,
When far-off matin bells were slowly ringing;
I have heard great Paderewski pound the keys,
But the pretty Harvey Girl, as I'm a sinner,
Produced the blithest of all melodies
As she clicked the plates while handing me my dinner.

—SE Kiser

Right: **The Harvey House in Hutchinson, Kansas. What a change from the greasy beaneries in the early years of railroad dining!**

Another point in Fred Harvey's favor was that he always allowed customers sufficient time to eat, without disrupting train schedules. Twenty-five minutes may not seem like much time for breakfast, lunch or dinner, but with the organized, efficient Harvey service it was sufficient time to ensure enjoyment of the meal—and it was a far cry from the five or 10 minutes allowed at the dirty, crooked beaneries of days past. Split-second timing, with the participation of the train crews, was necessary to allow this phenomenon of relatively leisurely eating on the railroad.

Before a meal stop, a brakeman went through the cars, asking passengers if they cared to dine and if they wanted dining room or lunch counter service. This information was wired ahead, so that the manager of the Harvey House would know how many people to expect and could plan the meal accordingly.

When the train was exactly one mile from the station, the engineer blew a signal on the whistle. An attendant—immaculately groomed, of course—stepped outside the restau-

rant and hit a gong once. At this sound, the waitresses placed the first course on the table. When the train stopped, the gong was hit several times and the passengers were seated. The other courses—steaks, ham and eggs, fish, chops and vegetables—were already cooking. After the first course, waitresses asked patrons what they preferred to drink—coffee, hot tea, iced tea or milk. They then placed the patron's cup in a special 'coded' position so that the Harvey Girl in charge of drinks would automatically know what to pour. If the cup was left right side up in its saucer, the patron was served coffee. An upside-down cup in a saucer called for hot tea. Upside-down and tilted against the saucer meant the customer wanted iced tea, and upside-down and away from the saucer meant he wanted milk.

At 15 minutes to the train's departure, an attendant gently told

Below: **Passengers on Sante Fe's *Navajo* enjoy the fresh air as the train glides through the rugged mountains of the Southwest. The next stop might be a Harvey House like the one *at right*—La Posada, the luxurious Fred Harvey Hotel in Winslow, Arizona.**

diners that there was no reason to hurry, there were still 15 minutes left. Time was called again at 10 minutes. Before the train departed, the conductor checked with the House manager to be certain that all customers were finished eating and aboard the train. Only then did the Santa Fe cars continue on their way.

For all his service and hospitality, Fred Harvey demanded only one courtesy in return from his customers—that the gentlemen wear coats to the table. Waitresses were instructed to ignore occasional 'boors' who made scenes about the rule. Although Harvey offered sober alpaca jackets in assorted sizes to coatless patrons, his insistence on this, to him, essential element of polite dining caused him more trouble than he expected.

In Oklahoma, for instance, Chairman Campbell Russell of the State Corporation Commission stoutly maintained that coat wearing was against Sooner custom. The Harvey House at Purcell thus refused to serve him. Russell and Harvey took the case all the way to the state Supreme Court. After long deliberation, Harvey's position was upheld. The court reasoned that civilization in Oklahoma was in a precarious position as it was, and influences in its direction should be encouraged. Besides, the court stated, if Harvey were ordered to serve men without coats, what would follow? Orders to serve men without shirts, or only in breechcloths?

Cowhands also frequently demanded to be fed coatless. In 1882, at the Castenada, a newly opened Harvey House in Las Vegas, New Mexico, some cowmen and their foreman rode into the dining room, shot off some bottlenecks, and, in loud and profane language, demanded a meal. Fred Harvey was present, and not for a moment did he lose his poise.

'Gentlemen,' he said, stepping forward, 'ladies dine here. No swearing or foul language is permitted. You must leave quietly at once.' They did, shamefacedly walking their horses from the room and carefully keeping the screen door from slamming behind them. The foreman later apologized for their behavior. To show there were no hard feelings, Harvey treated the cowpokes to a first-rate lunch, insisting, however, that his guests wear coats.

Only once did a brazen customer win his battle against the dinner jacket a rule. In Dodge City in the 1920s, Mayor 'Big Bill' Thompson of Chicago—a formidable, forbidding figure—led some cowhands into the dining room of Harvey's El Vaquero Hotel and demanded that they be served coatless. Thompson was an intimidating man. He had recently challenged King George V to fight him barefisted in the Chicago Stadium. In any event, he got his cowhands fed, though the scornful glances of the Harvey Girls somewhat withered their bravado.

Below: **The elegant dining room at the Harvey House in Kansas City, Missouri. In addition to fine food, Harvey wanted his customers to enjoy their meals in pleasant surroundings.** *Right:* **Even after World War II, Fred Harvey cuisine was one of Santa Fe's major drawing cards in advertising the fabled** *Chief.*

Smiling Harvey Girls *(above)* **and delicious desserts and pastries** *(below)* **added to the pleasures of traveling by train.**

Harvey stopped at nothing to make his establishments' meals of both uniform quality and infinite variety. To provide consistently good coffee, for instance, he had the water at each of the houses analyzed. Then he had special blends and mixtures developed to cancel out whatever effects the local water would have on the coffee's flavor.

Until Harvey added a little interest to menus, it was the custom to feed railroad passengers whatever was available locally from the region they were leaving. Thus, passengers on trains out of Chicago were fed Lake Michigan whitefish and Illinois corn; in Kansas City, there were steaks; trains out of California were supplied with seafood and fruit. Harvey changed all this. Of course, he had the advantage of using the freight service free from the Santa Fe, so by using refrigerator cars, often run at the head of the passenger trains, Chicagoans headed for the West Coast dined on California specialties before they got there; eastbound passengers enjoyed Kansas City steaks in the middle of the Mojave Desert.

The Harvey Company also cleaned up the act of the 'candy butchers'—candy sellers who walked from car to car on board trains, offering snacks and reading material. Harvey gave them good fiction and newspapers to sell besides the cheap pulp fiction to which they had been limited. He also supplied them with higher quality sweets. Sales rose impressively—by 1921, they were 60 times what they were when the Harvey Company was offered control of the service.

In addition to this service, the Harvey Company was also given the opportunity to branch out into the drugstore business. It began with one at the new Union Station depot in Kansas City, and when this proved a great success, the company opened drugstores in Chicago, Cleveland, St Louis and Los Angeles. But the company did not spread itself too thin. It was the very fact that it gave these stores as much attention as any giant hotel that made them a success. In 1921, Harvey's son told the story:

'When the new Union Station in Kansas City was about to be finished a few years ago, we were offered, along with the restaurant and other concessions there, the chance to run the station drugstore. If it had been a question of running an ordinary, good drugstore, we would not have been interested. We had never been in that business and we would not have cared to go into it for any such volume as we could have counted on.

'But when we looked into the possibilities of making it, in some respects at least, a more than ordinarily serviceable drugstore, we were decidedly interested, and we took over the lease.

'We proceeded as nearly as possible in the spirit of the Florence Hotel. Take a minor line, like perfumery, for example. We stocked, in this railway station drugstore, just about as comprehensive an assortment as you can find on State Street or Fifth Avenue or anywhere. There was no possbility of its paying its own way any time soon, and we did not expect it to—any more than the walnut furniture at Florence was expected to pay its extra cost soon.

Above: **Harvey Girls in Hutchinson, Kansas, circa 1900.** *Below:* **A Harvey Girl on duty at the lunch counter in Amarillo awaits the next crowd of hungry travelers.**

'But we did expect the perfume line to please people. We expected it to make a good impression, not only for itself but for the rest of the store. We expected it to set them talking about it and causing other people to come see it. And after a while, on its own account, as well as by boosting sales in the rest of the store, we expected it to pay.

'And it certainly has not disappointed us. We do a larger business in this one, ordinarily trifling line, I am told, than many prosperous drugstores altogether. Which, of course, is saying nothing of the effect on sales in the rest of the store, which has been considerable.

'We have not specialized in all lines to the same extent, by any means, but in every department of the store we have strived in some way to exceed the service expected, even though it could not be done at an immediate profit.

'The results have more than justified the policy. Before taking on the store, we got estimates from half a dozen experienced drug men on the volume we were likely to do. Our volume last year was six times as large as the largest of the estimates.'

When dining cars appeared, Harvey took charge of the Santa Fe's. Even though the kitchens were now moving on wheels, the cuisine and service were of the same high Harvey standard. The pride and joy of the Santa Fe system was the dining car on the *California Limited*, an all first-class express between Chicago and Los Angeles, which laid on meals to rival those in the finest European hotels—for one dollar. A typical dinner on the *California Limited* consisted of eight courses: grapefruit; olives, salted almonds and radishes; consommé; filet of bass with cucumbers; lamb chops à la Nelson, with broiled fresh mushrooms; roast turkey with cranberry sauce, mashed potatoes and cauliflower; salad; and plum pudding, cakes, ice cream, cheese and/or fruit, and coffee. By the 1930s, faster trains had cut down the need for railroad side stops, and two-thirds of Harvey's service was in dining cars, although some Houses were reopened briefly during World War II.

Stewards of these cars were encouraged to take a personal interest in their establishments. For instance, Bill Gardner, steward on the Kansas City-Chicago run, devised a '1001 Dressing'—an improvement on Thousand Island dressing. If a passenger liked it, Gardner presented him or her with a personal card containing the recipe. This was exactly the kind of service Harvey loved, and the kind of service that gave his system its reputation.

It was kept up, too, after Harvey's death in 1901, by his sons. First Ford, then Byron (after Ford died in an aircraft accident in 1928), headed the Harvey system, trying never to waiver from their father's standards. In the early 1920s, for example, the bottom fell out of the cattle market, leaving many cattlemen— frequent Harvey patrons—smarting from their losses. They were most upset and resentful to find that Harvey restaurants had not lowered the prices for their roasts and steaks. They were getting less money for their cattle, they reasoned, so restaurants must be paying less money for their beef. In fact, it was lower prices for beef by-products and cheap cuts of meat, which Harvey Houses never used, that drove down the price of cattle. The Harvey Company was paying as much as ever for fine steaks. But rather than lose the good will of so many of their customers, the Harvey system cut the prices of its roast and steaks to the point where they made no profit on them at all—and kept the cattlemen coming in. The move was considered well worth the temporary profit loss.

Right: **The El Navajo Hotel in Gallup, New Mexico—one of the many fine Fred Harvey establishments that were once commonplace throughout the Southwest.**

World War II made things difficult for the Harvey Company, as it did for many of those involved with the railroads. Food rationing, the necessary moving of thousands of servicemen, much of the labor force going off to war—all of these factors could make even the most well-run system creak and strain. But the Harvey system saw it through. Many former Harvey Girls came out of retirement to help serve the trainloads of soldiers that descended from the cars three times a day. Byron Harvey, then head of the enterprise, placed a gentle ad in magazines and newspapers, explaining the difficulties to civilian patrons. The ad closed: 'Fred Harvey hospitality, like a lot of other good things, may be temporarily lacking. Thank you for understanding why and being so patient and good-humored about it. When this war is won we promise you again the Fred Harvey service you have learned to expect.'

In its nationwide ad campaign, the Harvey system also utilized the character of a Private Pringle to explain the problems of wartime catering. Unknown to ad developers, there really was a Private Pringle. His first name was Murray, and he wrote Bryon Harvey that he liked the ads fine, was now a corporal, and could Mr Harvey please get him a dinner date with Lana Turner when he got back to the States? The Harvey system promised to do its best, but there is no record of whether or not it succeeded.

In 1943, the Harvey system served over 30,000,000 meals, of which 8,000,000 were served to the armed forces. Food fed to travelers and soldiers included 512,000 pounds of coffee, making 20,480,000 cups; 662,000 pounds of butter; 1,117,000 gallons of milk and cream; 1,250,061 pounds of sugar; 2,423,400 pounds of flour; 4,616,400 pounds of potatoes; 956,840 pounds of fish; 2,493,595 pounds of poultry; 5,172,835 pounds of meat; and 1,408,184 dozen eggs.

Wartime dining cars experienced as much of an increase in patronage as the Harvey Houses. On Santa Fe trains such as the *Scout* or *Ranger*, it was normal to feed 350 people in one 36-seat dining car, which meant the staff had to work through 10 30-minute seatings. At one breakfast on the *Scout*, the fry cook fried 1004 eggs in one pan.

After the war, however, railroad passenger business began to drop off dramatically. The public's preference for flying or driving on the nation's new concrete network of highways ate into even the Santa Fe's celebrated passenger service. The Fred Harvey Company was sold in 1968 to Amfac, Inc, a Hawaii-based corporation. Santa Fe passenger service was surrendered to Amtrak in 1973.

By the time it was sold, the Harvey Company owned some of the biggest, most beautiful hotels in the Southwest. The El Tovar, for instance, was one of the most expensive hotels in the country, charging $4 a day, when it opened. Built on the very rim of the Grand Canyon, it was also one of the most luxurious, more of a resort than a hotel. Nearby was the Bright Angel, where small, cozy cottages and camping facilities could be rented at lower prices. The Harvey subsidiary of Amfac, Inc still runs the hostelries and facilities around the Grand Canyon.

Some of the lovely Harvey Houses are now serving other uses. The elaborate La Posada at Winslow, Arizona is now part of the Santa Fe Railroad divisional offices there. A Harvey House in Belen, New Mexico is now a senior citizen center. These charming buildings are what are left of an empire that once offered a warm welcome, fine eating and good cheer to millions of weary travelers.

Every Fred Harvey House and Hotel was uniquely designed to match its surroundings, as can be seen in the elegant Southwestern motif at the La Posada lunch counter *(left)* in Winslow, Arizona and the warm, rustic interior of the Hotel El Tovar *(overleaf)* on the Grand Canyon's south rim.

THE DINING CAR

Just as railroads expanded in the mid-nineteenth century, so too did the amenities that they provided for their customers, and this had a great deal to do with ushering in the golden age of rail travel. In the early days passengers either brought their own food in boxes, or sometimes the train stopped so they could eat at station restaurants. The food was always terrible, usually black coffee made once a week, dry, salty ham, questionable eggs fried in rancid grease and put between slices of stale bread.

The first diner—a baggage car containing a counter and high stools—was put in service in 1862 on the old Philadelphia, Wilmington & Baltimore Railroad (later part of the Pennsylvania system). Its menu was oyster stew, crullers and coffee. Five years later, George M Pullman installed his first eating car, the *President*, on the Great Western Railroad in Canada. It was a 'hotel coach,' which was a sleeping car equipped with a kitchen. A year later his first diner in the United States, the *Delmonico*, went into service between Chicago and St Louis on the Chicago & Alton line.

In the 1880s, railroads began using diners as a means of building good will. Some of the old wooden diners had ornate chandeliers, potted palms, rubber plants and other flora sitting in elaborate vases in niches along the walls. The menus and prices were utterly astonishing by current standards. A typical dinner menu on a Chicago to Omaha train included: sirloin, tenderloin, porterhouse or venison steaks, prairie chicken, snipe, quail, golden plover, blue-winged teal, woodcock, broiled pigeon, mallard, widgeon, canvasback or domestic duck, wild turkey, veal, mutton, chicken, roast port, sixteen relishes, eleven clam and oyster dishes, five fish dishes, fifteen kinds of bread, many soups and desserts—any or all for 75 cents.

As late as 1907, the New York Central's dollar breakfast started with fresh fruit and baked apple, a choice of oatmeal or shredded wheat, Lake Superior whitefish, broiled or salted mackerel, choice of tenderloin or sirloin steak, ham or bacon, mutton chops or sausages. Another course was broiled chicken on toast with fried mushrooms, five styles of eggs, six of potatoes, an assortment of breads, wheat or buckwheat cakes, preserved fruit, marmalade, coffee, cocoa, milk or English breakfast tea.

Below: **The elegant dining car of Southern Pacific's *Shoreline Limited* and the kitchen *(right)*, circa 1900.**

rrier & Ives chronicled the wondrous and mundane moments on American life in the nineteenth century. A train ride on the Hudson River Valley line was a little of both.

PASSENGER RAILROAD DEVELOPMENT IN THE LATE NINETEENTH CENTURY

By Emory Johnson

In 1880 there were 93,296 miles of railroad in the United States, and in 1890 there were 163,597. In a single decade, 70,000 miles of railroad had been built in the United States. This marvelous achievement was unparalleled in the economic history of any other country of the world. Within 10 years, the people of the United States built as many miles of railroad as the people of the three leading countries of Europe had constructed in 50 years!

The building operations were carried on in all sections of the country, but the largest increases were made in the central and western states, where settlers were rapidly taking possession of the unoccupied agricultural and grazing sections of the vast public domain, and where vast mineral wealth was causing cities and states to be established on the great Rocky Mountain plateau. Capitalists, confident of the growth of the country and assisted by generous aid from the United States and from local

governments and individuals of the sections to be served, constructed railroads to create the traffic upon which the earnings of the roads must depend. In many cases, the railroads built during the 20 years following the Civil War were pioneers entering unsettled regions beyond the Mississippi and Missouri rivers and opening the highways by which immigration was able to rapidly occupy the prairies and mountain valleys of the West.

After 1890 railroad construction was not as rapid — completing less than 30,000 miles for the decade ending in 1900. It seems that by 1890 the most urgent needs for railroads had been met and that the country had been so well covered with the railroad net that only minor extensions were necessary.

Below: **Michigan Central Engine 191, circa 1880. The turn of the century marked the beginning of an era of passenger train improvements and refinements. The chandeliers, potted plants and leaded windows on the Southern Pacific Observation Car** *(at right)* **are typical amenities of the period.**

Above: **George M Pullman (1831-1897). He was a small town cabinet maker who moved to Chicago to seek his fortune. By 1870 his name had become synonymous with the luxury sleeping car.** *At right:* **One of George Pullman's creations.**

In 1906 there were 222,000 miles of track in the United States, nearly 40 percent of the railroad mileage of the world. The mileage in the United States exceeded that in all Europe by more than 15 percent. By 1929 the total mileage had increased to only 229,530, and by 1939 it had decreased to 220,915. Thus the turn of the century truly marked the point at which America's railroads turned from expansion to management of existing lines.

The improvements in travel and traffic resulted quite as much from the progressive adaptation of the vehicle itself to the service to be performed as from betterments in the roadbed and the locomotive. The passenger coaches first used were similar to the stagecoaches. Carriage builders, in making vehicles for the railroad, followed the designs with which they were familiar. Indeed, the passenger coaches of Europe, with their compartments entered from the side, indicated that the stagecoach influenced their style. Coaches of the European type were used on a few of the early American roads.

The construction of coaches for American railroads, differing totally in design from those used on highways, began with the opening of the first lines. The first railroad coaches had been not unlike the caboose in appearance, but after 1840 longer vehicles, mounted on two four-wheeled trucks, began to be used, and the typical American coach soon came to differ from the European coach. It was longer, had the doors at the ends and had a central aisle. This form of coach was probably adopted because the curves in American tracks required the use of trucks under the cars as well as under the engines.

Many improvements in design were necessary to produce the comfortable coaches that became the standard after about 1890. Better ventilation was secured by raising the central half of the roof and inserting 'deck-lights.' This was first done in 1836, but it was several years before the raised roof became a feature of all passenger cars.

The sleeping car originated with George M Pullman, who built the *Pioneer A* in 1864. Cars had been fitted up with tiers of

bunks on each side as early as 1837, but the discomforts of such accommodations were so great that sleeping cars did not become popular until the Pullman and Wagner services became available. The sleeping car was soon followed by the buffet or hotel car, drawing room and dining cars. The necessity for passing from one car to another suggested the vestibuling of trains. The idea was as old as 1852, when a man by the name of Waterbury first designed a vestibuled car. Some individual cars were fitted with vestibules that year, but the first vestibuled train was designed and built by Pullman and was run on the Pennsylvania Railroad in 1886.

In the United States, *passengers* in the nineteenth century did not divide themselves into classes as was customary in most foreign countries, but the railroads furnished different grades of service corresponding in a general way to the classes found on foreign roads. Most of the travel in America was on first-class tickets, but most companies also sold second-class tickets. On the routes over which travel justified them, excursion and immigrant trains were run which provided inferior accommodations at rates cheaper than second class. Beyond first-class accommodations were those furnished in the parlor cars and sleeping cars, called extra-fare cars.

Most American railroad companies, unlike those in foreign countries, placed the sleeping, parlor and dining car services in charge of a separate company. The Pullman Palace-Car Company —founded by George M Pullman—owned and operated most of the cars in use from the beginning of this service in 1865 until 1955.

For many years, the Vanderbilt-controlled Wagner Palace-Car Company of Buffalo built and managed from one-fourth to one-third of the sleeping, parlor and dining cars. In 1899 these two companies consolidated under the name of the Pullman Company, which controlled nearly all the extra-fare cars. The Chicago, Milwaukee & St Paul, the Canadian Pacific, the Great Northern, the New York, New Haven & Hartford systems, and a few other companies, ran their own cars exclusively, but their total numbers were relatively few.

The railroads paid the Pullman Company mileage (about one cent per car mile at the turn of the century) for the use of the coaches, and the Pullman Company, in addition to this revenue from mileage, received the extra fares paid by the passengers for the privilege of riding in the parlor or sleeping car. On some especially fast trains, the railroads charged more than the usual first-class fare, to cover the additional expense of running the trains at high speed.

The parlor and sleeping coaches were much heavier than the ordinary first-class day coach, and had accommodations for fewer people; hence the profits received by the railroads from the parlor and sleeping car traffic were really smaller than those obtained from the day coach service. Someone said that 'The man who sits up all night in the day coach helps pay for the fare of the man who rides in the Pullman car.'

The railroad companies found it to their advantage to rent the parlor and sleeping coaches instead of owning them, because the Pullman Company, having control of a great number of cars, was able to supply the railroad with just the number of cars required. When one railroad company or one section of the country had a large demand for coaches, some other company or section probably didn't need more than the usual quota, and the Pullman Company was able to distribute the cars economically according to the needs of the service.

Right: **A Canadian Pacific passenger train pauses at Glacier House in British Columbia. Note the Colonist Sleeping Car on the left.**

THE RUN OF THE SCOTT SPECIAL

By Frank Newton Holman

At one o'clock in the afternoon of Sunday, 9 July 1905, a special train, chartered by Walter Scott, pulled out of the La Grande station of the Atchinson, Topeka & Santa Fe system at Los Angeles.

A few minutes before noon on Saturday, 8 July 1905, a man by the name of Walter Scott walked into John J Byrne's private office in the conservative Life Building in Los Angeles. Mr Bryne was the Assistant Passenger Traffic Manager of the Atchinson, Topeka & Santa Fe lines west of Albuquerque. The stranger wore a cheap serge suit, a blue woolen shirt, high-heeled vaquero boots, a cowboy hat, and a fiery red tie. He pitched the hat into one corner of the office, tossed his coat on a settee, and, dropping into a chair, remarked quietly: 'Mister Bryne, I've been thinking some of taking a train over your road to Chicago. I want you to put me there in 46 hours. Kin you do it?'

Mr Bryne whistled.

'Forty-six hours?,' said he. 'That's a big contract, Mr Scott. That is 11 hours and 56 minutes faster than the eastbound run has ever been made. Man, do you realize that half the road is over mountain divisions?'

'I ought to,' answered Scott. 'I've been over the Santa Fe 32 times between here and Chicago. I ought to! Here's the money!' And the man in the blue shirt began to shed $1000 bills.

'I'm willing to pay any old figure, but I want to make the time! Kin you do if for me, or can't you? Let's talk business!'

Mr Bryne drew out his pencil, and as he figured he talked. The miner broke in every few minutes with a shrewd remark. The conference lasted a long time, and in the end Bryne put the $5500 in his safe.

The train had been bought and paid for.

'Young man,' said Bryne, 'the Santa Fe will put you into Chicago in 46 hours, if steam and steel will hold together. We've got the roadbed, the equipment, and the men; don't forget that. But let me tell you that you'll be riding faster than a white man ever rode before!'

'Pardner,' said Scott, simply, 'I like your talk. it sounds good to me. Line 'em up all along the way and tell 'em we're coming.'

An hour before the time appointed, the *Coyote Special* was standing in the depot of the La Grande station in Los Angeles. Thousands of curious sightseers were on hand to see the miner start on his wild ride for a record. As the time drew near, the crowd increased until the train sheds were packed and from every eminence faces looked down.

A big engine slowly backed up and wheezed into place at the head of the train. The train consisted of engine number 442, baggage car 210, dining car 1407, and the standard Pullman car *Muskegon*, three cars weighing exactly 170 tons. This was the train which came to be known as the *Death Valley Coyote* or the *Scott Special*.

A big automobile dashed up to the entrance of the station and Walter Scott alighted. He had to fight his way through the crowd to get to the train. Entering the cab, he shook hands with the engineer, greeted the fireman, and, urged by the crowd, made a short speech from the tender.

In the meantime, the party who were to accompany him had boarded the train. Mrs Scott, a comely young woman altogether without nerves, awaited her husband in the Pullman. CE Van Loan, the newspaper representative who was to write the story of the run, busied himself with his typewriter, and the writer hereof completed the quartet.

At last the clock pointed to the hour, No 442 gave a warning toot, visitors scrambled off the train, Conductor George Simpson raised a long forefinger and the *Coyote* began to move. A great cheer went up from the spectators. Scott waved his slouch hat in response, and inside of fifteen seconds the *Coyote* disappeared from sight.

The passage through the city was a fleeting ovation, crowds lining every street to see the train dash along. The little towns outside Los Angeles flitted by like shadows, the cheers of the crowds shrilling an instant and then dropping away from the tail of the racing train.

Thirty-five miles out of Los Angeles, the jar of the air brakes told that something was wrong. The big engine was slowing down and, high on the flank of the mountain of steel, a fireman was clinging.

'Too bad!,' said Conductor Simpson, 'The tank box has gone hot on us! The fireman's playing the hose on it.'

But the trouble was immediately rectified and then the train began to whiz in earnest. Engineer John Finlay meant to make up that lost time. And he did. One hour and fifteen minutes had been the railroad schedule to San Bernardino. The *Coyote* cut 10 minutes off this time. Here a helper engine was picked up, and in a few minutes the engine-drivers were attacking the heavy grade of the Cajon Pass. Up near Summit, at the crest of the hill, we saw the first bit of what, to the amateur railroaders of the party, seemed almost miraculous railroading. A mile before we reached Summit, the helper engine was uncoupled on the fly and, while the speed of the train never slacked for an instant, the light engine dashed ahead, ran onto a siding, the switch was thrown back, and the oncoming special whirled over the crest of the hill.

Here it was a different story. We were on our first descending grade. The problem now was not how fast we could run, but how fast we dared run. So we shot down toward Barstow at a mile a

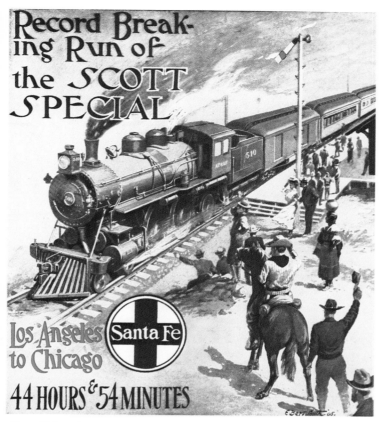

Record Breaking Run of the SCOTT SPECIAL

Los Angeles to Chicago

Santa Fe

44 HOURS & 54 MINUTES

Above: E Bert Smith painted the cover for the original edition of Frank Newton Holman's account of the run of Walter Scott's *Death Valley Coyote.* He put Teddy Roosevelt on horseback viewing the train, but, in fact, the President was in the White House when Scott telegraphed him from Dodge City that 'An American cowboy is coming East on a special train faster than any cowpuncher ever rode before: how much shall I break transcontinental record?'

After the run, 'Death Valley Scotty' retired to the Mojave to live in a castle he built there, which in turn became a famous resort known as, of course, 'Scotty's Castle.' On nearby Interstate 15, motorists watch their speedometers hover at 65 and dream of Scotty's 84 mph dash across the desert.

minute, turning and twisting in and out, Engineer Finlay's hand always on the air-brake. When we made the mile between mileposts 44 and 43 in 39 seconds, or at the rate of 96 miles an hour, we began to feel that the great race was fairly on. Fast time on a mountain division is a very different proposition from the same rate on the straight-away of the plains. Mountain divisions are full of curves, and if one pauses to reflect on the impact with which 338 tons of equipment hits the outer rail of a sharp curve when hurled against it at the rate of 90 miles an hour, the charm of record-breaking is often tinged with the pale cast of thought. Personally, I am glad that I did not have time to think of these things while they were happening. It is much wiser not to inquire too curiously into such matters until afterward. Meanwhile, the certainty that your welfare was the thought uppermost in the cool brains of every member of the operating department of the Santa Fe system compares not unfavorably with the comforts of a clear conscience. At any rate, it supplements them nicely.

Back in the Pullman, we knew that every man who had our safety in his keeping had been picked with reference to his known possession of the qualities which make for security as well as speed—safety first, then speed. And so, when they told us that we were skimming their roadbed faster than a train had ever done it before, we patted the Santa Fe system on the back and said:

'Hit her up!'

We whistled into Barstow 26 minutes ahead of the killing schedule which had been laid out for us. That 26 minutes was the gift of Engineer Finlay and his crew, and anyone looking for

good railroading may rely on them to repeat it as often as the call comes in.

At Barstow we changed engines for the race across the desert. It was a warm run from Barstow to Needles, but the *Coyote* took it on the fly, causing the lizards to hastily hunt their holes and making the cacti by the roadside look like a hedge fence.

At 7:13 the Colorado River shimmered in the distance; at 7:17 the *Coyote* came to a standstill at the head of the rail yard at Needles. In exactly eighty seconds, the train was moving again, a fresh engine taking up the work. Thousands lined the track near the depot, but they had no more than a fleeting glimpse of the flying special, and she was gone.

Twelve tortuous miles below Needles, the Santa Fe crosses the Colorado River on a steel cantilever bridge—a marvel of modern engineering, flung solidly across a wide, tawny stream. Engineer Jackson swung over that twisting track at 65 miles an hour and the glasses leaped in the diner. A rush of sound, a creaking of bridge timbers, and with a dull whirl the *Coyote* found Arizona soil.

To quote verbatim from a dispatch to the *Kansas City Star*:

Have you ever seen the salt cellars playing ping pong with each other? It is not conducive to a healthy appetite. One gets to wondering what would happen if an engine should take the ditch going at that rate of speed. The correspondent looked over at the conductor, Tom Brayil, and it was great relief to an amateur record-breaker to note that he was still smiling. 'Jackson don't know a curve when he sees one,' called the conductor across the car. 'The whole road looks straight to him.'

Here is the menu of the *Death Valley Coyote*, eaten at sixty miles an hour over a mountain division:

Caviar Sandwich a la Death Valley; Iced Consommé; Porterhouse Steak à la Coyote (two inches thick) and a marvel of tenderness; Broiled Squab on Toast, with Strips of Bacon au Scotty; Stuffed Tomatoes; Ice Cream with Colored Trimmings; Cheese; Coffee; and Cigars.

Now, where can you beat that, Mr. Epicure? Hats off to Chef Geyer, who will see the trip through to Chicago. Mr Geyer has been many years in the service of Fred Harvey, and when he was slated to make this run, his wife objected seriously. She reminded Geyer of his four small children and bade him let some other man break his neck on the *Coyote Special*.

Any man who can cook like that at 60 miles an hour is worthy of a place in the culinary hall of fame.

Three hours of hard mountain railroading brought us to Seligman, where we picked up an hour. Division Superintendent Gibson climbed into the Pullman, and his first facetious words were: 'What detained you?' Jackson's daredevil run will go down in song and story as the most spectacular dash of the western section.

Then began the real fight of the trip—a war against heavy grades. Clouds of sparks whirled by the windows—the little Arizona towns winked once as the *Coyote* passed. It was here, they said, that we were to win or lose, for if we could make the schedule up and down the divides which separate Seligman from Albuquerque, win over the famous Glorieta Pass, and hold our own on the Raton Mountains, the record was ours beyond question.

It is impossible, recalling the events of that nerve-wracking night, to pick out for special mention the names of the railroad heroes who won for their road a victory over those grim Arizona mountains.

I only know that from time to time crews of stern-visaged men succeeded one another; that engines were changed in record haste, and that Division Superintendent Gibson, heavy-jawed, laconic, and resourceful, rode the train, alert, confident, and conquering. Outside, the cool mountain wind swept through the stunted pines, and over all twinkled the clear stars of the great Southwest.

There was no sleep on board the *Coyote* that night. In far-off cities tireless presses were reeling off the story of the flying *Coyote*, and on board the train Van Loan hammered away at his staggering typewriter, clicking off the tale of the run which now belongs to railroad history.

It was not until the first switch at the outer edge of the Albuquerque yards clattered beneath the flying wheels that Superintendent Gibson smiled.

'I've brought you over the Albuquerque Division 34 minutes faster than any train ever went over it before,' said he, as he bade us good-by. He had beaten the time of the *Lowe Special* by 34 minutes; he expected to beat it by 30.

The two Indian villages between Albuquerque and Lamy had never seen a train dropped down a hill at such a rate of speed. Engineer Ed Sears was at the throttle, and every inch of the track

is well known to this big engineer. A helper engine swung in at Lamy for the climb to the top of the Glorieta, one of the steepest grades on the entire run, 158 feet to the mile. Back in the Pullman, Trainmaster Jim Kurn grinned as he greeted Scott.

'Here's where you get a touch of real mountain railroading,' said he, 'and we're going to beat the schedule if we have to sidetrack that dining car. She's got another hot box.'

'Sure,' said Scott. 'If she smokes any more, cut 'er out!'

A few minutes later, the *Coyote* struck the Apache Canyon, a wild bit of mountain country, memorable as the scene of many an Indian fight. At the rate of 40 miles an hour, the train climbed the incline. There were a few seconds of delay as the helper engine dropped out, and then began the 'real mountain railroading.'

Down the steep grade Sears drove his engine, the white mileposts flashing by at the rate of one every minute. The whole train lurched and staggered over the reverse curves, the typewriter carriage banged from side to side, and the passengers, looking at each other, smiled. It seemed that the train must leave the track as it took those great curves, and from the diner came a man, blanched almost white. It was impossible to stand up in the leaping, swaying Pullman. One man tried to stand it; his shoulder went through the window. After that, we were all content to sit still and hang on. Only Jim Kurn was calm. He knew Sears'

Below: **Hell bent for steam en route to Dodge City, a Santa Fe passenger train over takes the Butterfield Overland Stage. It marked the passing of an era as the Scott Special crossed Kansas in nine hours at a speed of 85.5 mph.**

reputation for careful running, but it seems to me the engineer crossed the limit hard that morning. None of us were sorry when the train stopped at Las Vegas.

At Raton, Jim Kurn said good-by.

'You're a long way ahead of that schedule now,' he said, 'and it won't be our fault if the people east of here don't shoot you into Chicago on time! It's hard work fighting these mountains 23 hours out of every 24, but show me a mountain railroad man who wants a job on a plains division! Good luck!'

Two engines took the *Coyote* at Raton. The time of the change was a trifle over a minute and we were off again. 'Hud' Gardner is another mountain engineer who knows the game. He brought us into La Junta at 5:13, hours ahead of schedule, and the worst part of the journey was behind us.

East of La Junta lies the Santa Fe 'racetrack.' It is here that trains are supposed to make time. With a straight track, the Kansas plains lying level as a floor and a good roadbed underneath, the *Coyote* took up the second part of the journey.

With engineers Lesher, Simmons, Norton and Halsey alternating in the cab all the way from La Junta to Newton, the new and mighty balanced-compounds whizzed down the Arkansas Valley. 'Scotty' rode the engine into Dodge, with the telegraph poles looking like a fine-tooth comb. It was from Dodge that he wired President Roosevelt:

'An American cowboy is coming East on a special train faster than any cowpuncher ever rode before; how much shall I break transcontinental record?'

All that Monday night the miles flew from under the whirring wheels—in places at the rate of 85 and 90 miles an hour—the average for 300 miles being a mile every 50 seconds. The great Kipling once wrote the story of a record-breaking run East over this same road. It is part of his *Captain Courageous*. It was fiction, but it reads like fact. That is because Kipling wrote it. On almost every point covered in his narrative of the fictitious run I can say he tells the truth. He says, however, that 'The ties ripple and surge away behind the flying train,' and for once he is wrong. Given a reasonably straight piece of roadbed, the faster the train goes the smoother it goes. And the ties do not ripple and surge away behind it. The roadbed just slips away, as the paper slips from the roller of a big newspaper press. That was the way it slipped from under the wheels of the flying *Scott Special*.

Josiah Gossard, who has been an engineer on the Santa Fe for 23 years, took the train from Emporia to Argentine in the quickest time ever made between those two points—124 miles in 130 minutes, notwithstanding four slow orders and several grade crossings. Gossard has a medal, recently presented by the Shriners, for making up one and a half hours of lost time on their special, Newton to Kansas City.

It was nearly 8 o'clock Tuesday morning when the *Coyote* crossed the Mississippi. The end was almost in sight now.

We had taken on another engineer at the Ft Madison repair shops, just on the western edge of Illinois. He was a German named Losee. As a fine finisher in the stretch, you will look a long time for his equal. Stolid, modest, destitute of nerves, he is the direct antithesis of the daredevil engineer of fiction.

With Losee at the throttle and a straight-away stretch to the wire, the *Coyote* cut loose for the run home across the state of Illinois. They knew all about 'Scotty' and his private train in Illinois. And so they made a holiday of that July morning, and every little hamlet along the line from Shopton to Chicago turned out to cheer the *Coyote* on to the goal.

It was one ovation all through Illinois. And Losee was earning every bit of it. The special had made some splendid miles in Colorado and Kansas. She was to outdo them all in Illinois. Losee ran engine No 510 from Ft Madison to Chillicothe, 105 miles, in 101 minutes, changing at the latter point to clear track into Chicago, with every switch spiked and the entire operating department standing on its toes 'rooting.'

'Scotty' rode a part of the distance on the engine with Losee, and helped the fireman feed coal into the furnace.

From the little hamlet of Cameron to the still smaller one of Surrey is 2.8 miles. 'She' made it in one minute and 35 seconds, at the rate of 106 miles an hour. The world's record before had been held by the Pennsylvania road, which covered the 2.5 miles between Landover and Anacosta in 102-miles-an-hour time. That was in August 1895.

We lost five minutes at Chillicothe, and four more at South Joliet. Nevertheless, we made the run of 239 miles from Shopton to Dearborn Street station in Chicago in 239 minutes.

At 11:54 on the forenoon of 11 July, *The Coyote* came to a stop in the Dearborn Street station, Chicago, having made the run of 2265 miles in 44 hours and 54 minutes. The record stands unparalleled in railroad history.

The best previous run between these points had been made by the *Lowe Special* over the same road in August 1893, which covered the distance in 52 hours and 49 minutes. The latter train, however, ran westbound and carried only one baggage and one Pullman car. The best previous record on the eastbound run was made by the *Peacock Special* in March 1900, Los Angeles to Chicago, over the Santa Fe, in 57 hours and 56 minutes, carrying a Pullman sleeping car and a buffet/smoking car.

The story of this latest epoch-making feat of railroading was told graphically in the public press. From edition to edition its details leaped into large type in the newspapers, were caught up and passed from lip to lip, the whole continent catching the sporting spirit of this mad dash from the Pacific to the Great Lakes.

To the general public it meant, in the main, the freak of a speed-mad miner; to railroad men the run of the *Coyote* was a matter of much more engrossing interest. Many of them did not sleep while the train was on the road. It was not the thrilling spectacle of a blue-shirted daredevil shaking hands with death, delirious with delight in danger, that kept them tense. It was the growing joy of the accomplished fact, the steady conquering of the seemingly impossible, the imminent fulfillment of careful calculations—something, too, of the sobering sense of an unusual responsibility.

Left: **In the footsteps of the *Scott Special*: Santa Fe's eastbound *Grand Canyon* running around a freight train in Cajon Pass, where the main line crosses the coast range of mountains.**

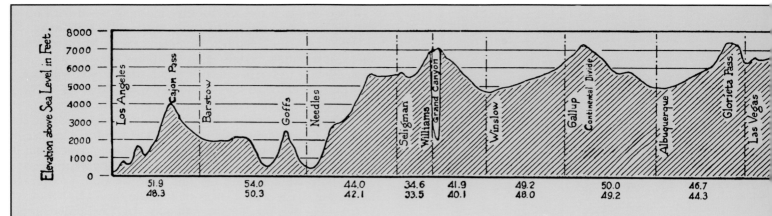

Condensed Profile of the Santa Fe System, Los Angeles to Chicago.

Note: The upper row of figures below the profile shows the average speed in miles per hour made by the Scott Special in the various districts not including delays. The lower row shows the average speed including all delays.

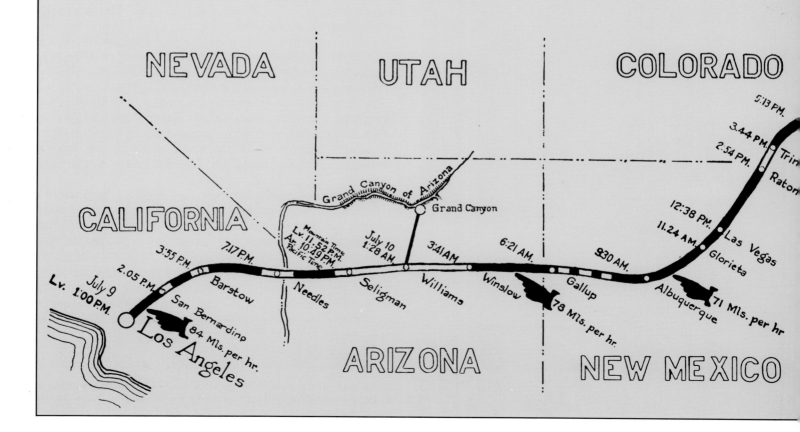

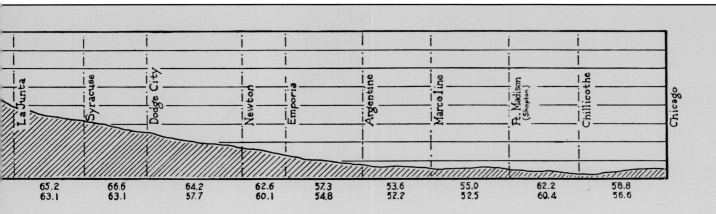

	La Junta	Syracuse	Dodge City	Newton	Emporia	Argentine	Marceline	Ft. Madison (Shopton)	Chillicothe	Chicago
	65.2	66.6	64.2	62.6	57.3	53.6	55.0	62.2	58.8	
	63.1	63.1	57.7	60.1	54.8	52.2	52.5	60.4	56.6	

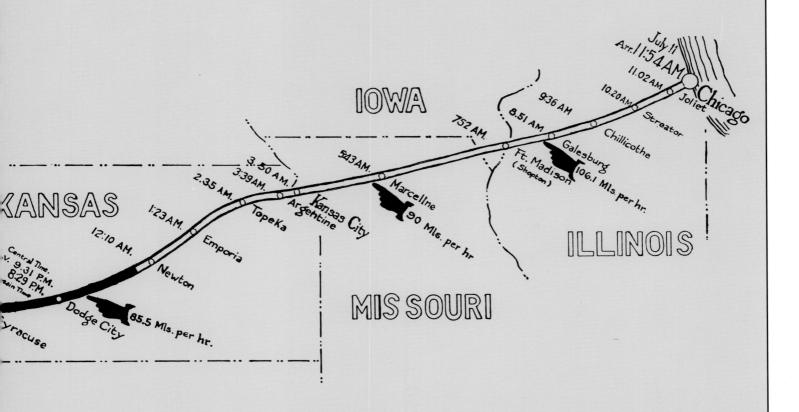

Map Showing Run of the Record-Breaking

Scott Special Train

consisting of

Baggage Car 210, Dining Car 1407, and Pullman Car "Muskegon."

Total Car Weight 170 tons.

Left Los Angeles 1:00 P.M. July 9, 1905.— Arrived Chicago 11:54 A.M. July 11, 1905.

Distance 2265 miles.   Time 44 hrs. 54 min.

Average Speed per Hour, 50.4 Miles (including all delays)

WHEN EVERYBODY CAME BY TRAIN

1900-1939

PART TWO

WHEN EVERYBODY CAME BY TRAIN

By Bill Yenne

In the United States the frontier era had ended in 1890 — Congress even went so far as to officially declare such. In Canada, it was much the same situation, and the North American people breathed a sigh of relief and looked toward the future.

The first four decades of the new century were characterized by both boom and bust—by enormous prosperity followed by a deep depression. Yet, through it all, the trains were there, a thoroughly integral part of American life and civilization.

The railroad *companies* may have diminished in stature but the *railroads* remained. Gone were the great rail barons of the nineteenth century, who lit their hand-rolled cigars with hundred dollar bills. The iron horse was now *everyone's* steed.

Below: **Contented passengers aboard a Santa Fe club car in the 1920s. Gone are the days when travelers would sit back and relax, with cool drink in hand, amid the comforts of the club car as the country rolled past.** *Right:* **A mother and daughter at the Southern Pacific Station in San Francisco about to set off on a fun-filled journey one spring morning in April 1938.**

Those decades were an era of isolated innocence before the big war, a time when the great expansion was over and the new world was enjoying the fruits of a tamed continent. Incredibly, over 90 percent of the rail lines that would be built upon this continent already existed by 1900, so the notion of traveling by rail was a common part of everyday life.

The mournful sounds of a train whistle in the wide open spaces of America's plains and deserts have been an integral part of American folklore since the nineteenth century, but by the 1930s those whistles had become a permanent national icon, a haunting, inescapable, essential part of the American collective consciousness.

On the rails of America in those halcyon days of the 1920s and 1930s travel was so reassuring and so intimate. It was not the unreal, soporific and precarious aloofness of a plane, nor that obsessive simulacrum of resort life one finds on today's ocean liner. The relaxing periodicity of the incessant clickety clack of rails, the immediacy of scenery masquerading as something more *itself* than just an abstract, geometrically-shaped land mass, the utter determinism and variety of a fixed, impervious route through changing climates and seasons—all these conspired to lullaby one's will within and into its own private heaven.

It was as though the apotheosis of that assassin in all of us, that would do away with space and time and remove all obstacles together with their attendant anxieties, was calm at the controls, while at the same time furious in the engines. Aboard a train one felt that the *forces of nature themselves* were conspiring to make sure that one was always getting nearer, nearer. One sensed moment to moment that one knew where one was going. It was only when one stepped off that one was lost again, and life became uncertain.

Above: Penn Station, New York: They were the temples of their era—the vast, cavernous train stations built to handle the masses as they crisscrossed the nation. Though still filled with the hustle and bustle of people moving from here to there, something has changed—gone is the innocence and security of another time, another place. *Right:* The smoky moodiness of a late autumn run through Shawinigan, Quebec on the Canadian National.

In his 1939 essay, *I Travel By Train*, Rollo Walter Brown describes traveling in the dead of night in the Oklahoma Panhandle country. He climbed aboard a long train from the Pacific Coast that had generously offered to stop at a small town for a solitary passenger. Brown was still awake from a busy evening, and while the porter made down a berth for him, he wandered back through the train—through two or three darkened sleeping cars, where passengers, snug behind green curtains, were sound asleep, then through four or five others that were almost as dark, but not made down for the night, and without passengers. In the rear section of the last of these a brakeman—a man of forty or forty-five with an 'active' face—sat musing in the dim light of the berth lamp. The unoccupied cars, he explained, had carried a company of youngsters to a Conservation Camp farther southwest, and were now going 'deadhead' back to Kansas City.

For five minutes Brown stood and talked with the brakeman.

'Sit down,' he begged of Brown at last. 'I haven't talked to anybody all day.'

The experience of rail travel in the 1920s and 1930s encompassed a spectrum that ranged from the hot dustiness of the baggage room *(below)* to the cool crispness of a first class compartment. In the scene *at right*, which could have—or perhaps should have—been conceived by Maxfield Parrish, mother and daughter share a quiet moment amid the splendor of silk, silver and enameled stainless steel.

'He seemed a trifle loquacious, and it was late, but I complied,' said Brown, 'and as soon as we were seated, the brakeman laughed a little. 'I wanted to get you down so as I could ask you a question. If you don't mind, I'd just like to know what you work at. When you came walking back here I hardly thought you looked like a businessman.'

Brown let him guess, then told him.

'Well, say! A writer?' replied the brakeman. 'I don't often meet any of them—that is, that I know of. But I know a book you or somebody ought to write—about trains and railroads and the excitement of them.'

Brown told him that he was soon to go to work on a volume that might not be altogether unlike what the brakeman had in mind; and that for more than a dozen years he'd had to cover much of the United States three or four times each year, and that he intended to write about what he had seen—about a trip here and there out of many.

'But you'll be sure to say plenty about trains, won't you?' replied the brakeman. 'Anybody that ever saw as much water as the Cimarron River has got in it in August writes about ships. Trains are lots more thrilling. Ever stand in the Union Station at Cincinnati or St Louis, or in one of the big stations at Chicago or Minneapolis, at night maybe, when the big boys with their

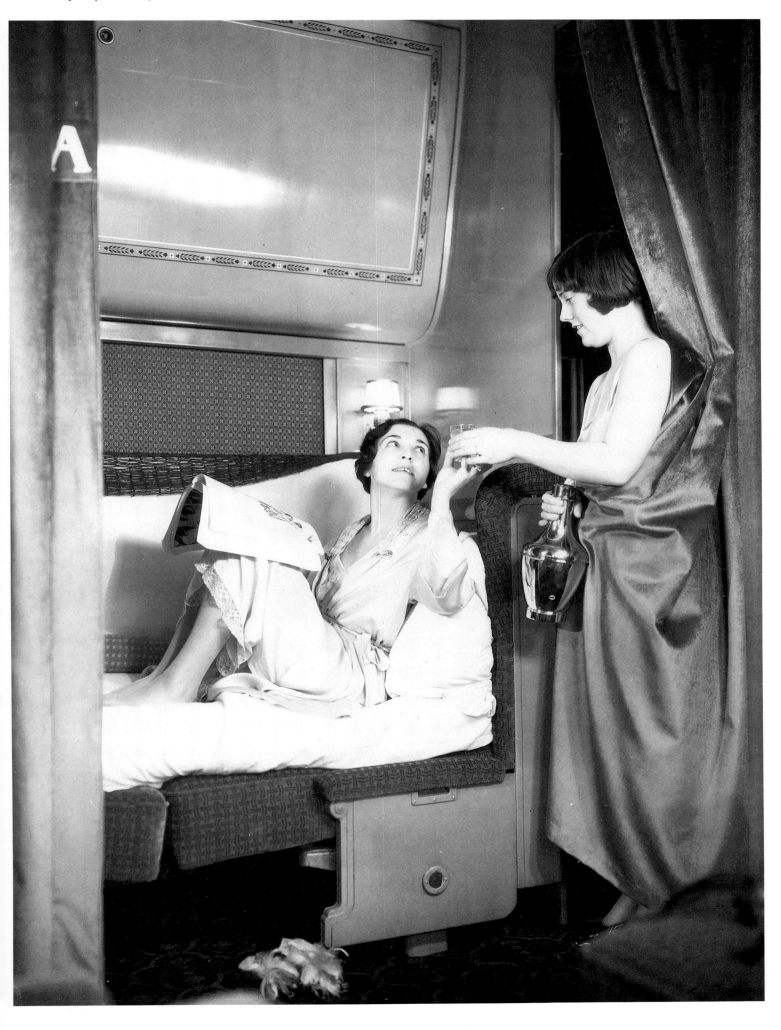

names on their tails are all lined up to go—the *Bluebonnet*, the *Chief*, the *Corn King Limited*, the *Katy Flyer*, the *Viking*, the *Meteor*, the *FFV*, the *Flamingo*, the *Wolverine*, the *Zephyr*, the *Columbine*, the *Golden Arrow*? You see, I know some of them, all right.

'And boy! You don't go to sleep while you're working on a train. Can you imagine what it's like jumping off the pilot of a freight engine to run ahead to open a switch, and your feet slip out from under you where there's some smooth ice under the snow, and you fall smack across the rail with the old engine creeping along only about eight feet behind you? Or when everything is covered with ice, slipping down, ka-plump, between two flat cars when they're moving? I did that once starting on a night run to Omaha. I had sense enough to keep on running, down in there between the two sets of trucks, but she was already going too fast for me to dodge out across the rails, and I didn't know how long I was going to be able to keep on running, with the engine picking up a little all the time. Then she began to slow down, and finally stopped! "*Boy, oh, boy!*" The engineer said his engine didn't feel as if she was pulling just right, and he thought he'd better stop and find out what was wrong before he got going. Now isn't that good enough for a book?'

'Yes,' replied Brown, 'but you are the person to write that one. Mine will be about the people I see on trains—what they are up to, and—'

The brakeman interrupted, saying 'I could write one like that, too—if I knew how. I talked once with fourteen movie actresses on this run. And sometimes I see something along the way. There! In that little town the agent's wife is a sour-looking devil—I know that much.'

Brown tried to pull him back to his point of view. He told the brakeman that he was interested in the people he saw when he got *off* trains, too, in the people who produce food, in the people who must go hungry, in what people endure, in what they dream, in what comes true—and in what it all seems to mean when you try to put it together.

'I get you!' he said. 'The lowdown on everybody.'

'No,' Brown protested. 'It would be a story of the United States, which one long distance train traveler had eventually come to see and think about.'

In *I Travel by Train*, Rollo Walter Brown did in fact discuss the people and places he *reached* by train, but among his most vivid recollections are those concerning the *process* of train travel itself. A typical recollection involved a trip to Washington, DC which began in an Ohio hill town in the bleakness of January. When Brown arrived at the station, the ticket agent offered to put the bags inside his office, if he wished to feel free of them. The agent would see that they were up on the platform when the train arrived.

'If they're not in sight the minute you get up there yourself, don't worry,' he said. 'They always wait, you see, till I tell 'em to go.'

'I walked out into the raw cold,' Brown recalled. 'The air promised snow. Two or three blocks away the tower of a court-house built in the President Grant era of architecture was trying to express the newer spirit through twinkling lines of incandescent lights that ran in every direction over it as if it were advertising a carnival. It provided something to walk to and I struck off in that direction.

'Almost as soon as I had climbed the stairs to the long covered platform, a piercing beam of light shot athwart a slight curve to the westward on the edge of the town; and before there was time for the agent to do more than rush up and say, 'Here they are;

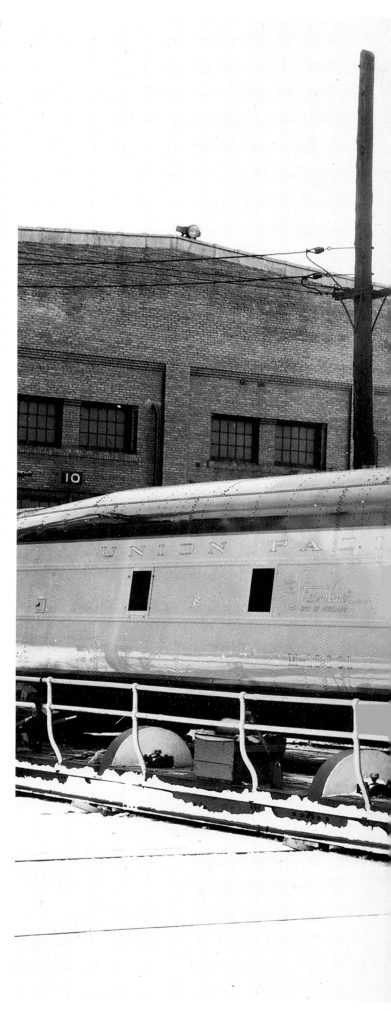

Below: Harbinger of a new age of diesel motive power wrapped in the stainless excesses of high art deco, the Union Pacific's *City of Portland* streamliner was introduced in 1935. There was snow on the ground when Rollo Walter Brown *(see text)* left Omaha.

Overleaf: Rail travel was indeed a taken-for-granted part of American life when this photograph was made at the Southern Pacific ticket office in the lobby of San Francisco's Palace Hotel early in the twentieth century. In 1923, President Warren G Harding would die upstairs from this scene (some whispered murder) and would be borne back to Washington DC—on the train!

he usually opens her up about here,' the towering dark hump of a locomotive that suggested unlimited power by its ease of motion shuddered by, and a brightly lighted train of fifteen cars or more came to a stop.

'Right on here,' the Pullman conductor suggested, 'if you don't mind, and walk back through, so we can hustle along. I'll have your porter come up and get the bags.'

Brown had to walk almost the entire length of the train. 'After the dull light of the street and the station platform, the brightness was dazzling. There were sleeping cars in which the berths had not yet been made down for the night filled with cheerful people who seemed not to have a care in the world; a lounge car filled with other cheerful people—mostly women—who were the least bit boisterous in their drinking; a dining car filled with yet others who dined well; and other standard sleeping cars and bedroom cars with affluent looking luggage and passengers in every berth and open bedroom.'

Rollo Brown cleaned up a bit, dug a book from one of his bags and started toward the dining car. 'Yes, went up two points,' a man was saying as Brown passed his space.

In the dining car, the steward squeezed him over to an unoccupied chair next to the window—and next to a sizzling hot steampipe. The other three at the table were two women and a man who were returning from California. After they had ordered, Brown picked the book up from the window ledge and began to turn to the place where he had left off.

A trip to Mardi Gras on the Southern Pacific might have included a stop at Houston for a quick lunch in the station's modern cafe (right). There was room at the counter with a cheerful staff to serve you, and plenty of tables.

'There was a moment of silence as if the three had discovered a strange breed right at the table with them. Then one of the women asked, "Oh, what was that book I meant to read on my way back? I had forgotten all about it. I wonder where it is." Otherwise, nothing much was said. The women exchanged a few words of disappointment over Hollywood, and the man grunted once or twice. When he grunted the second time, one of the women admonished him: "Well, what did you read the newspapers for if you didn't want to know whether stock had gone up or down?" '

After they left, the three new ones who took their places had not yet decided what they would have beyond their cocktails when Brown was ready to go.

As Brown walked on to the smoking room at the other end of the car, the porter was already making down the berths. The smoking room was deserted, so he dropped down into the corner of the long leather seat and went on with his reading.

Brown heard voices approaching. 'The trouble with this damned country,' the loudest voice was saying just as somebody pushed the green portiere aside, and men—five of them eventually—began to file in, 'is that everybody who has anything left is being taxed to death for these reliefers.'

Brown slid over close against the wall, and soon the five of

Below: **Decked out in mink and silk ties, happy first class travelers regard the photographer from the fantail of the club car on Southern Pacific's Overland Limited as it heads over the famous Lucin Cutoff across the Great Salt Lake in Utah. The cutoff, which was completed in 1903, consisted of 16 miles of rock-filled causeway and 12 miles of wooden trestles.**

them were in complete possession, with cigars slightly elevated, as if there could be no possible doubt about anything that anybody in the group chose to declare.

'My God!' the chief speaker went on. Then he smoked avidly as if an idea were just beyond the end of his cigar. 'We've got to stop paying relief, that's all.'

'All right!' Brown said, and slapped his book shut with enough decision to make a bit of a report and startle them into seeing that somebody else was present: 'Let's begin next Monday morning. I've just been down in a coal region that I know pretty well where a thousand miners have been squeezed out of work by the installation of improved mechanical equipment in the mines. Now what are you going to do with them next Monday morning?'

'Next Monday morning? Oh, my God! Give us a little… Give us six months.'

'But you can't have six months. These men and their families must have something to eat next week.'

The other four smoked and looked toward the floor out in the center of the room, but their spokesman squinted at me, turned his cigar over in his mouth a time or two, and then demanded: 'Say, are you a socialist?'

'Why? Does a man who believes that people ought not to starve have to be a socialist?'

'Well,' and he squinted his eyes and the whole of his big face into deeper lines as if he were trying to think and to be amiable at the same time, 'it always looks a little suspicious, doesn't it?'

Brown's berth was toward the other end of the car, and when

he went to it with the thought of reading in bed, the porter and the Pullman conductor were having an argument with a man of thirty or thirty-two about his ticket. He sat on the edge of the freshly made-down berth with a good sized flask beside him, and drank away a bit unsteadily from a paper water cup as if he were trying to ignore everybody about him. Two young women sat on the edge of their berths across the aisle and drank with slightly more self-command from the same kind of cups. A stately gray-haired woman stood by the Pullman conductor.

'Well, let me see your ticket then,' the conductor was demanding. 'This lady says this is her berth that you are in.'

'I'm not in her berth—wouldn't think of such a thing. It's my berth—*Number 12*. That's what my ticket said, and that's all there is to it. These young ladies here were right across the aisle from me in *Number 11* and *Number 9*—have been ever since we started. Right there, *Number 11* and *Number 9*. That's what it says, if I'm any good at reading. I asked them to go forward with me and have a drink or two and we did. When we came back we decided to have another, and I got this of my own here out of the bag, and so we've been having it. Now what's wrong with that?'

'I'm sorry, sir,' said the conductor, trying to be impressive, 'but I must see your ticket stub.'

'I'm sorry, sir,' the drunk replied, very successfully mimicking him, 'but I can't let you. Why, I paid for this berth —*Number 12*—and I'm on my way over to New York to relax a little, and that's all there is to it.'

'But this car doesn't go to New York; it goes to Washington.'

The drunk fished in his pockets and found the stub of his Pullman ticket. 'There you are, sir' he said triumphantly. 'Doesn't that say *Number 12*?'

'Yes, but *Number 12* in the second car up ahead.'

He made a pass or two before his eyes, as if he were puzzled. Then all became clear: 'How could that be? These two young ladies were right across the aisle from me when I got on, and here they are right across the aisle from me now. So who's right? Tell me! Who's right?' 'Let me see your ticket stubs,' the conductor asked of the two girls.

They found them.

'Sure!' the conductor assented. 'They are up in the other car, too.'

Suddenly his face revealed greater bewilderment than ever. He picked up the flask, looked at it as if he now for the first time, noticed something alien about it, looked at the bag that stood open on the white sheets of the berth, put the flask back in, stood up with all the formality he could command, bowed deeply—as deeply as was safe—to the stately old lady, and said like a man of the world, 'I am very sorry; I beg your pardon.' Then as if he had thought of something bright, he added, 'But it was very good!' and followed the young ladies forward.

Sometime late in the night Brown awoke without being aware of any special reason. He tried to picture the train somewhere in the middle of Pennsylvania. He tried to think only of how comfortable the trip was, as he was lulled by the steady purring buzz of the air conditioner in his berth. He listened to the deep roar of the train. 'Sometimes it is pleasant to do that—while the serpentine, miniature world to which one has entrusted one's self

for the night sweeps like some dim, earth-fettered comet through dark hills, over mountain ranges, and down into broad valleys. But a train roaring along through the night is no place for a man who has been taking final leave of anybody.

'I thought the roar seemed muffled. I pushed the shade up without snapping on the light, so that I could see into the darkness outside. We were gliding along the Susquehanna River, and snow was descending without bluster in great, substantial flakes. I let my forehead and nose rest against the cold glass of the window and watched. There is something very decent about snow.

'A moment or two and we were taking the sharp curve onto the picturesque, many arched stone bridge above Harrisburg. Five minutes later we were creeping through the snowy maze of tracks just outside the station. Men worked—a small army of them—with shovels and brooms and picks and torches and oil, trying to keep ahead of the snow, trying to have every switch in working order so that it could be thrown. As I saw them out there from my berth, they appeared to work in absolute silence. All over the eastern United States men like these were out at three or four in the morning, had been out all night, keeping tracks cleared and switches working so that people could have a good sleep while they were getting to Washington or New York or Philadelphia or Boston. What if some of them should grow careless and some switch—the one ahead of us for instance—should not close? It was good to see them working so painstakingly out there, drawn together in cooperation by a mighty need.'

Another of Rollo Walter Brown's vivid descriptions of train travel in the late 1930s involves his taking the Friday afternoon *Lobby Limited* from Washington to New York. The two men and the woman who sat at the luncheon table with him in the dining car were returning from a brief holiday in Florida, but they had spent a couple of days in Washington, where the men had to see somebody about something.

'You know I think it's an awfully clever idea,' the man in the sky-blue shirt and double-breasted coat declared. 'He says that all he needs now is the taste. You see, it's an established fact that dogs like scraps from the table better than any dog food that has ever been invented. Well, he has a marvelous food —simply marvelous—but the dogs still prefer the scraps because of the taste. He has more than twenty—think of it, more than twenty— research men at work on the problem of the taste—PhDs from Harvard and Cornell and everywhere. If they can find the taste to put in the food that will make the dogs prefer it to the scraps, why his fortune is made. You see how it will be: every woman in the country will chuck everything from the table into the garbage can and *buy* food for her doggie. It would help business, too.'

'I could have contributed a word to the conversation,' Brown said to himself, 'for I had visited a laboratory—possibly the one they had in mind—where the best brains of the country were at work on the same problem. But when I glanced up as if I might speak, nobody's look included me, and I remained content to listen.'

When it seemed that nothing more was to be gleaned, Brown walked back through the train to the observation car. Every chair was taken—even the one at the writing desk. Men with wide open eyes and relaxed cheeks inclined toward each other, made sweeping gestures with hands that held half-empty tall glasses, and spoke with great positiveness as if no word they might utter should be missed.

In the singing roar of a train that was making 70 or 80 miles an hour, and the incessant sharp lurches of the rear car as the rest of the train made a whipcracker of it, Brown caught only occasional words—'General Motors'—'If we could only get him'—'New England Power'—'Tel and Tel'—'Nickel Plate.' The man who sat right at my knees in a low-slung chair where I stood by the door was almost in tears. 'God, think of that! If it had gone through, he would have cleaned up two million dollars!'

Brown walked forward through the train till he came to a smoking room in one of the older style parlor cars. A man of early middle age who looked as if he lived much of the time out of doors sat smoking a pipe and reading a journal on architecture.

'You're the first man I've seen on this train,' Brown told him without fearing the consequences of interrupting him, 'who seems to be interested in anything essential.'

He took his pipe from his mouth and looked up as if he had not been at all taken unawares. 'I thought I was the only one—till just now.'

He moved over in suggestion that Brown sit down and they talk. Always the sarcastic critic of society, Brown wanted to know whether one could devise 'some giant perforated flapjack turner that would let all the solid productive people go down through and hold the soft parasites on top, and if one were to heave the fluff into the Atlantic Ocean, how many people would be left?'

'In the region of New York, not enough to start the subway tomorrow morning!'

The architect laughed. 'Oh, it wouldn't be quite so bad as that. As a matter of fact, we have more mills and legitimate commer-cial agencies in New York than we get credit for having. But I'm afraid if you carry your experiment through there'll be a lot of empty offices downtown and up around Murray Hill.'

One is reminded, of course, of Zimmerman's words—also penned in New York—where he asked, 'Name me someone who is *not* a parasite, and I'll go out and say a prayer for him!'

They talked all the way into New York. 'Come and have a bite to eat with me, and we'll finish,' he suggested. 'I'm a bach. We can drop your luggage at your hotel, and go right on over to mine.'

Up in his room on the thirty-second floor, after Brown was through with a hot tub and was ready for the quiet reading, he discovered that one of his bags—a small Irish kit bag—was not there. In its place was another, of the same size and color. He called the porter and told him that one of the boys had been careless. The hotel porter was very positive. 'There had been no carelessness. He did not permit any. The bags were the ones put out of the cab.'

So Brown called the Pullman Company's Lost and Found office and 'Some realist in this office answered the telephone.' He suggested that it might have been a three-cornered trade—that the owner of the bag, Brown, had might not be the man who had Brown's at all. Anyhow, the chances were that he was on his way to Montreal or California by this time.

The hotel's house detective, an ex-Marine, came up.

'We'll go through it,' he said simply. 'We might find a clue.'

They did find a clue, and by midnight Brown was on his way

Ticket takers like the ones *below* at the Houston Station in 1934 would have greeted passengers as they traveled through the Southwest crossing the country via Southern Pacific's Sunset Route.

out to an address in the region of 204th Street in uptown Manhattan, where he recovered his lost bag.

In the observation car on the way home, two men who held tickets for Providence and talked about the easy money they believed could be made pretty soon now, drank so many times to the health of two women who had chanced to sit at the luncheon table with them, that 'They almost changed their plans for the entire weekend.' When the women got off at Westerly, however, the two men insisted that Brown come over and join them.

'Couldn't they see that I was up to some nice little game, myself? It was written all over me. And what especially did I think of the state of the nation? So much depended on that. When I told them—perhaps with too much guile—that we seemed to be in need of some thinking—a little thinking—one of them said—the one who was in the rubbery state: "But the trouble with the damned country is that we people who use our heads are so hopelessly in the minority—the submerged five percent, you might say. Isn't that so?"'

'Whenever I think of traveling,' wrote Rollo Walter Brown as he departed Concord, New Hampshire in October 1937, 'I see the United States as merging areas of color. For I always begin my travels in the autumn. It was so a year ago; it was so the year before last. The day of departure carried its own announcement. Chill winds swept across the New Hampshire hills from Mount Monadnock and whirled the showering maple leaves everywhere. The last lingering bluebirds sought the protected side of the barn and chirred regretfully in the afternoon sun. Shining pheasants, a dozen strong, marched boldly into the open meadow, stopped, and while the wind almost blew them off their feet, looked toward the house as if to say, "What? You still here?"'

'By the next morning I was without regrets at going. For the wind had left the hills only dull, colorless pinnacles that were rendered all the more desolate by occasional areas of evergreen and clumps of birches the least bit too white in their fresh nakedness. Down on the edge of Massachusetts the maples still provided a little color—until you came too near—and in Concord and Arlington and Cambridge there were almost as many yellowing leaves on the elms as in the streets beneath them.'

Brown was going cross country on this occasion, and thought a section in the sleeping car would be more comfortable for so long a journey. Across the aisle a boy of six and his mother adjusted their belongings for a trip as far as Newark, Ohio. 'The mother was not a Bostonian; she had only married one. I like children,' Brown mused, recalling proudly how he had always been able to work with children playing—though not fighting—right beneath his window in Cambridge. 'A little girl in front of

---

A commercial traveler asked the porter to put him off at Buffalo, where the train stopped in the small hours of the morning. 'And I'm apt to be cross,' said he, 'when I'm waked up in the night. I might even fight. But don't pay any attention to my objections. Put me off.'

Late in the morning the traveler awoke at Schenectady. He sought the porter in a rage.

'Why the ding ding didn't you put me off at Buffalo, as I told you?'

The porter's eyes rolled and his jaw dropped. 'Gee, who you suppose it was that I put off at Buffalo?'

Right: A Southern Pacific schedule heralds the arrival and departure of the locals that once conveniently and comfortably crisscrossed the San Francisco Bay Area. These routes are gone now, and commuters are forced to depend on buses or cars.

SOUTHERN SAFETY PACIFIC

ARRIVAL OF TRAINS

DATE Mar.. 2 nd.

FROM

	DUE	Will Arrive
OGDEN ROUTE		
"PACIFIC LIMITED" All Eastern Points.	8.00A	X
"SAN FRANCISCO LIMITED" Denver Salt Lake City Ogden Reno.	8.40 "	X
"St. LOUIS EXPRESS": St.Louis Kansas City Denver Ogden	10.22 "	X
FAST MAIL	12.02 P	
"OVERLAND LIMITED" All Eastern Points.	12.55 "	
SHASTA ROUTE		
SAN FRANCISCO EXPRESS–Seattle Tacoma Portland Ashland Klamath Falls.	7.00A	X
"OREGONIAN" Seattle Tacoma Portland Ashland.	9.35 "	X
CALIFORNIA EXPRESS–Seattle Tacoma Portland Ashland.	6.15P.	
"THE SHASTA" Seattle Tacoma Portland	9.35 "	
LOS ANGELES AND SAN JOAQUIN VALLEY		
OIL FIELDS PASS–Bakersfield Porterville Visalia Fresno Martinez.	7.35A	X
"OWL": Los Angeles Bakersfield Fresno	8.25 "	X
"TEHACHAPI" Los Angeles Visalia Fresno Los Banos Merced Tracy via Martinez	1.40 P	
SUNSET EXPRESS–New Orleans El Paso Los Angeles Porterville Fresno.	7.00 "	
"VALLEY FLYER" Bakersfield Fresno Modesto Los Banos Tracy	10.15 "	
SACRAMENTO AND SACRAMENTO VALLEY		
Truckee Colfax Sacramento Davis Benicia Port Costa.	8.00A.	X
Truckee Colfax Sacramento Benicia Port Costa Richmond.	8.40 "	X
	9.35 "	X
Dunsmuir Gerber Davis Benicia Port Costa.	10.22 "	X
Colfax Sacramento Benicia Port Costa.	11.03 "	X
Sacramento - Davis - Suisun - Benicia - Port Costa	11.20 "	X
Sacramento & Way Stations.	2.42 P	
Oakdale Stockton Tracy Newman Los Banos Livermore Pleasanton Niles	3.20 "	
Gerber Corning Orland Willows Williams Woodland.	3.20 "	
Sacramento Davis Benicia (Vallejo) Richmond.	6.05P	
"THE STATESMAN" Sacramento - Davis - Suisun Fairfield	6.15 "	
Dunsmuir - Red Bluff - Marysville - Sacramento - Benicia	7.00 "	
Stockton - Tracy & Way Stations via Niles	8.20 "	
Sacramento Davis Elmira (Rumsey) Benicia (Vallejo Sunday Only)	9.25 "	
Dunsmuir - Red Bluff - Chico - Marysville - Sacramento - Davis - Suisun Fairfield	9.25 "	
Gerber Corning Orland Willows Williams		
VIA VALLEJO OR MARTINEZ		
Martinez Vallejo Pinole Richmond & Way.	8.05A	X
Tracy - Pittsburg - Bay Point - Martinez - Napa - Vallejo	9.45 "	X
Port Costa Crockett Vallejo Rodeo Pinole Richmond.	12.25P	
Santa Rosa Calistoga Napa Martinez Pt.Costa Vallejo Richmond.	5.40 "	
Avon Martinez Port Costa Vallejo Junct. Selby Rodeo Pinole Richmond.	5.56 "	
Ship Yard Train Bay Point. [Daily except Sunday]	6.40 "	
Tracy. Bay Point. Martinez, Richmond.	11.25 "	
LIVERMORE AND SAN JOSE VIA NILES OR NEWARK		
San Jose. Agnew. Newark. Centerville. Niles. Hayward. San Leandro.	6.42A.	X
San Jose & Way Stations via Niles.	7.40 "	X
"STOCKTON FLYER": Stockton Tracy Livermore Pleasanton Niles	9.43 "	X
Tracy & Way Stations via Livermore & Niles.	2.42P	
Santa Cruz Big Trees Los Gatos San Jose & Way Stations via Newark.	5.40 "	
San Jose via Niles.	6.00 "	
Tracy & Way Stations via Livermore & Niles.	7.00 "	

X—Denotes Train has Arrived.

TRACK 9

TRAIN NUMBER 46

SU SUN-FAIRFIELD ELMIRA
DIXON DAVIS
MARYSVILLE

Train travel in the 1930s as Rollo Walter Brown would have experienced it—Porters assist travelers *(above)* at the Third Street Station in San Francisco, California, and a few lone passengers *(left)* await the arrival of their train at Southern Pacific's station in Houston, Texas.

me smiled at me with great blue eyes 'round the corner of her high-backed seat. The boy saw her smile, and felt that he must participate. But he was less subtle. He walked over and wanted to know what my name was, and where I was going. His mother, who tried to look unadorned and sheer, very mildly reprimanded him.'

At Westerly a 'little, dried-leaf of an old lady, who must have been at least eighty-five,' came shakily into the car. As the train started, it tottered her into a seat on the wrong side of the aisle.

'Oh,' she exclaimed with a startling clearness, and rather eagerly, as if she were not always heard attentively, 'I didn't mean to do that. I want over there, on that side—where I belong.'

The very courteous, Black porter helped her over.

'Now!' she said. 'Now! Now I can see them when we pass. It is so comfortable, too. So if it wants to storm now'—the sky was a little heavy—'we'll just let it storm.'

Soon, a waiter came through from the dining car hammering out some musical notes every so often and announcing that this was the last call for lunch.

'A man can put in a lot of time in a dining car if he is experienced. He can order item by item as he eats, and then eat very slowly, with full pauses now and then to read two or three consecutive pages in some interesting book, and with other pauses for the passing landscape. So for an hour and a half I sat and ate lettuce salad, and belated blueberry pie and ice cream, and read a little, and reordered coffee that was hot, and looked out at the sea, and heard, without trying, the conversation of the two youths at the other side of the table who professed ardently to believe that their prep school had more class than either Groton or St Mark's. One of them had just bought a yacht for which he had paid more than I in an entire lifetime had ever earned—or at least had ever received.'

After lunch, Brown repaired to the observation car, and it was here, and in this context, that he recorded his thoughts, based on a dozen years of people-watching throughout the land.

'On the Boston to New York trains, as one walks through,' he observed, 'there are more people *reading books* than on *any* other trains in the United States. It must be said also that there are more feet stuck in the aisle, more people who glance up in disgust at you when you wish to put the aisle to other use.'

There were no unoccupied chairs in the observation car on this particular October day, so he immediately walked the full length of the train in the other direction. In the coach smoker, close up against the section devoted to baggage, he sat on the sleek oilcloth upholstery the rest of the way to New York, enjoying the bronzed reds of the Connecticut hills, the lighthouses on rocky points, the gulls flying everywhere, and 'listened with approval from some vague emotional depth of myself to two battered old pugs with heavy cauliflower ears while they declared with many variations that it was the good old sock right on the corner of the chin that made the world go round—at least for the other fellow in the ring.'

'Somewhere in the region of Hell Gate Bridge, the train moved hesitantly for a time, and then made a broad sweep southward as if it were trying to find a way of getting around New York. It was as though it was *exploring* as it sped along. As it circled into open space, one of the fighters—they had both been silent for a time—looked off to the west with a puzzled, interested stare as though he were seeing something that was beyond his understanding. Then I saw. The whole of New York from the region of 42nd Street on downtown stood up in a leaden sunset sky like the dream of some brilliant madman. In a moment everybody in the car was silent and looking. It was

Porters helped to make traveling by train even more enjoyable by helping passengers with everything from warming up baby bottles *(above and below)* **to giving advice and directions** *(opposite).*

something pagan, yet something unearthly. What had men been celebrating when they built it? A moment later, when the train carried us along slowly where a veil of smoke in the foreground subdued the fading sunlight even more subtly than the clouds in the background had, the gray of the towers was less of the Earth still. Soon afterward the train came to a full stop. There was no confusion near us outside, and everybody in the car was, for the moment, as silent as if he slept. We participated in something fantastic.

'Evidently the train decided that there was no way of getting around. The only thing left to do was to go under. It gave us a violent jerk, swerved sharply to the right, and made a dive into a roaring tunnel which eventually brought us into the bowels of the Pennsylvania Station.

'I went up for air. I bought the latest edition of three or four papers. I bought a magazine or two. I bought a book. And I received the welcome reassurance that New Yorkers are just as childlike as anybody else, by watching hundreds of them solemnly ride a newly opened escalator down, since they were not going at the end of the day in the direction that would enable them to ride it up.'

A great many of Brown's recollections involve travel to New York City. It is a clear testament to the power and magnetism that the great metropolis had over the Northeast—and indeed over the nation—in the era of American history preceding World War II. In those days, all roads—all steel roads—seemed to lead to

New York City, and Rollo Walter Brown—consummate traveler upon those rails—was led, again and again, to the great city. Nevertheless, he is remembered for having said that, 'It is never a journey until one is beyond New York. From New York it is still possible to telephone back home in a jiffy. And always among the pushing millions there are some of your friends. When I take a bedtime train in this direction I always find a vague inappropriateness in going to bed until we are past New York, at two o'clock or so. And if I do go, I do not feel that I can settle down to solid sleep until after the long stop and the quick coming of the tingling pressure in the ears as the train drops swiftly beneath the Hudson. But when we are beyond the Hudson we are away—regardless of the hour. We have left behind everything peninsular and known. We are facing something vastly expansive. The train moves as if it had plenty of room.'

The next morning when Brown awoke, the light was squeezing in at his window. He pushed the shade up to see where he was. The train was racing along a winding river among rounded hills, and two old women in sunbonnets fished from a flatboat. The maple trees on the hillsides beyond the river were as much green as yellow or red. When the train sliced off a piece of corn field to save the trouble of keeping to the river, the ground from

Many Pennsylvania travelers of the 1930s found their way to New York City. Upon arriving in that grand city, passengers would disembark at majestic Penn Station. *Right:* The Romanesque Main Waiting Room at Penn Station and the elaborately designed and spacious lunch counter *(below).*

which the corn had been cut was matted with white and pink and purple morning-glories—and the fences were covered.

The galloping train swung out into more open country. Far in the distance he made out a dark train as long as his own, and racing as swiftly. He could tell by the design of the cars that they were sleepers. As day grew bright, today and every day, how many of them were there, racing everywhere in the United States, carrying whole towns of people along in their beds—and preparing breakfast for them? He visualized a 'map of the United States with every long-distance train designated, as we mark the daily location of ships on the Atlantic. There they were, speeding everywhere—up from the South, across the Alleghenies, along the Great Lakes, down the Mississippi, across the Great Plains, through the Rockies, across the sands, up and down the Pacific coast.'

When he was dressed, fed and ready to leave the breakfast table, the train slowed down and was cut over to the eastbound track. A moment later they passed scores of 'foreign looking laborers,' who were busy putting down new steel on the track that normally would have been taken by the train on which Brown was traveling. Almost before they were at full speed again, there were wild shrieks of the whistle, and a 'jolting, shuddering grind of brakes which brought us to such an abrupt stop that tableware crashed to the floor.'

Since he had finished eating anyhow, he went to the nearest open vestibule to lean out and see what had happened. There were fifteen cars in the train, and the diner was in the middle. Brown could see the conductor hurrying along on the ground, from far in the rear, looking intently under the train as he ran. Far forward, the engineer, wearing clean-looking striped overalls, was coming back, looking under a bit more deliberately. Three

---

Thomas S McPheeters, one of the leading businessmen of St Louis and prominent in the work of the YMCA, frequently illustrated in his addresses that there was a common avenue of approach to the hearts of men by the following story:

My wife's mother—of whom I am very fond—had spent the winter with us at St Louis and, when she felt that she must leave, the duty of arranging for her transportation and the checking of her baggage fell upon me.

For some reason I failed to secure the check for her trunk from St Louis to her destination and secured only only a transfer check from the house to the station. On reaching the station, I found there were but five minutes before the train left, and in great haste I ran to the baggage room to exchange my transfer check for a through baggage check.

To my consternation I found the baggage room crowded by a multitude of importunate travelers, each determined that his baggage be attended to. My task seemed hopeless of accomplishment.

On the inspiration of the moment I stood up on a chair and shouted out so that everyone could hear, 'Gentlemen, gentlemen, this check is the check for my mother-in-law's baggage. If I fail to have it attended to in the next five minutes, she stays with me all spring!'

Instantly the crowd divided and a pathway was made for me to the desk and six baggage masters hurried to me with the cry, 'Let me help you!'

—Senator Selden P Spencer

During the heyday of passenger trains, countless baggage handlers like the ones *at left* attended to travelers' belongings, and the baggage always ended up right where it was supposed to be.

or four porters had swung down and were standing back on the turf so that they might see farther alongside.

Our literate traveler also swung down and walked forward toward the engineer. Before Brown had not quite reached him, he stopped, looked back toward the conductor, and with a single easy lift of his stout arm signaled for him to come on up.

'There he is, under the front trucks of that baggage-car,' the engineer said, not able to be wholly matter-of-fact.

The conductor steadied himself by putting one hand against the lower edge of the car's body—which stood high above the roadbed—and looked under. A black-headed boy of about four-teen lay there limp and almost completely nude from having been dragged and rolled over rough limestone ballast.

'He's not cut up to speak of,' the conductor said. 'We ought to get him out of there and be on our way in no time.'

From somewhere a representative of the railroad company appeared. He glanced under. 'That's easy. I'll look out for everything. You can scoot right along.'

From somewhere also—from the houses on the hillside just above the right of way—a number of dark eyed children came running to see why the train had stopped.

'Any of you kids know who that boy was that was walking on the tracks bringing groceries home from the store?'

A cloud swept the faces of the entire group, as if they thought the boy had been arrested for something that he should not have done.

'Do you?'

'Yes,' the oldest boy in the group said. 'It was Fortunato.'

'Fortunato? Your brother?'

'No, just my—friend.'

'Well, he was walking on the tracks, and the train killed him.'

In terror and helplessness the boy looked about at the rest of us as if we ought not to be there, twisted slowly away without moving his feet, lifted his hands to his face and then sank to the earth sobbing, 'Oh, Fortunato!'

The other children stood speechless, except one boy who said half to the rest, half to the conductor, 'The train was running on the wrong track.'

'Yes, I know it was. But you see, he shouldn't have been walking on either track. He should have walked in the road.'

'But there are automobiles.'

Brown wandered back along the train. As he passed the dining car it was still crowded with people who were obliviously enjoy-ing their breakfasts and the bright morning. He climbed back onto the train and walked all the way back to the observation car, where there was only one person—a stout woman all freshly made up for the day, who was busy with a story in a magazine called *The Delineator*.

She glanced up. 'Can you tell me why this train is standing so long?' she asked. 'We don't seem to be in any town.'

'Oh,' Brown replied, 'we killed an Italian boy up ahead.'

'Why, how perfectly terrible!' she said in a voice so well modulated that she might have been reading from the story.

The train gave a little shrug of a lurch forward. 'But I guess we must be going now.'

Passengers began to come in from breakfast. Soon they had filled all the comfortable chairs. For two hours Brown sat with his back to the window and read. Periodically, he let the book drop to the arm of the chair and looked out at the windows on the other side of the car past the heads of the solid row of those who sat across the aisle and did their own reading or smoked as if for

Right: This Southern Pacific gas-electric combo was used for short distances in the early part of the twentieth century. Though trains of this sort primarily provided passenger service, they were also used to transport cargo.

once it would do no good to be impatient. Groves of maples, numerous in the hills and on the flat land alike, were splashed with fire. Occasionally a tree was solid yellow. Why had nobody ever said anything about the beauty of the hills between Coshocton, Ohio—or Athens—and St Louis? Only Brown County, Indiana has received any part of the praise due the entire region. And Brown County became known chiefly because a group of painters found it paradise when the genteel population of neighboring cities laughed at it because it was short on railroads and plumbing.

Within the train, too, a change had taken place since the crossing of the Hudson. Most of the New Englanders had gone on to Washington—if they had not taken a boat at New York—and the transcontinental passengers had already been outnumbered by energetic Buckeyes, who are always going somewhere, and who 'are not troubled in the least by getting up and taking a train at 5:00 or 5:30 in the morning. They sat wherever there was room, smoked cigars, talked pleasantly with some half recognizable remnant of New England or Virginia in their speech, and felt that the world was not such a bad place, after all.'

As it came into the smoke of East St Louis, Illinois, the train moved cautiously above the housetops as though it was getting ready for something important.

'Old Man River!' a man from Kokomo, Indiana announced.

'I find something to come over here for every once in a while just to see this.'

There was quiet as the train moved deliberately above the last houses—'frowsy affairs of tarred paper, corrugated iron, and oddments of boards—and out over the east bank of the spreading river, over the resistless, eddying, boiling middle of it, where we could look down through the steel of the bridge into it just as if

> As she lay in her berth, staring at the shadows overhead, the rush of the wheels was in her brain, driving her deeper and deeper into circles of wakeful lucidity. The sleeping car had sunk into its night silence. Through the wet windowpane she watched the sudden lights, the long stretches of hurrying blackness. Now and then she turned her head and looked through the opening in the hangings at her husband's curtains across the aisle.
>
> She sat up stiffly, staring out at the dawn. The train was rushing through a region of bare hillocks huddled against a lifeless sky. It looked like the first day of creation. The air of the car was close, and she pushed up her window to let in the keen wind. Then she looked at her watch: it was seven o'clock, and soon the people about her would be stirring. She slipped into her clothes, smoothed her disheveled hair and crept to the dressing-room. When she had washed her face and adjusted her dress she felt more hopeful. It was always a struggle for her not to be cheerful in the morning. Her cheeks burned deliciously under the coarse towel, and the wet hair about her temples broke into strong upward tendrils. Every inch of her was full of life and elasticity. And in 10 hours they would be at home!
>
> —Edith Wharton
> from *The Journey*

Right: Great Northern's *Empire Builder*, one of the famous luxury trains of the past, carried passengers from Chicago to Seattle comfortably as well as quickly—The train made the run in less than 63 hours. The *Empire Builder* is seen here at the St Paul Union Depot on 11 June 1929, the day of her inaugural run. Great Northern continued its tradition of luxury travel with the introduction of the United States' first fleet of streamliners in 1947, and dome cars in 1955.

nothing much supported the train, and at last over steamboats moving in to the western waterfront.' Soon everyone scrambled forward to be ready by the time the train reached the station.

For Brown, St Louis was only a pause, and not even long enough to 'rob me of my sense of motion.' His next train stood ready, and he was on it so soon that he had difficulty in feeling that he had made a change.

After a late lunch, Brown sat in the lounge half of the cafe car and studied the world outside. Within two or three hours the train was climbing toward a ridge of the Ozarks—over sharp curves and counter curves, 'on and on, up and up. Close beside the long train, which moved a little below speed yet resistlessly, thin looking cows picked grass from steep, rocky hillsides under good sized papaw bushes that were just beginning to lose their greenish yellow leaves and reveal fat clumps of green fruit quite ready to fall.' Brown noted that the only bright color anywhere was the red of the gum or persimmon trees.

'How many railroads are there in the world,' mused an effusive Rollo Brown, 'that spurn the valleys, as this one does, and follow low mountain ridges for a hundred or a hundred and fifty miles? In these ancient, worn off hills the valleys were too complicated, too stuffy, for some dreaming surveyor, and he took to the hills. Now, after the engine's long, steady climb that seemed to be taking us across a county or two, we were up on them ourselves. We swept round long curves from which we could look down over ranges of hills on both sides of the train; we took long straight-of-ways on the comb of watersheds; we described letter Ss; we made sharp, hair-pin turns—all in an effort to keep to the ridges. Once we passed a freight train that was taking water at a tank and filling the air with surplus steam. Several minutes later I saw the same train not more than a mile or two from us across a wooded valley. We had followed a wide, round horseshoe in order to get where we were.'

Two men who shared the cafe car with Brown had been drinking steadily while they discussed the economic ills of the country. 'Their eyeballs were getting pretty yellow,' but they could still see what the train was doing. 'I bet you, by God,' one of them began easily, as if he were established in a point of view that enabled him to see whatever was wrong, 'that the fellow who had the contract for building this railroad got paid by the mile. Just look there, will you? There's that same damned freight train that we passed a half-hour ago. Why didn't they come straight across there? It wouldn't have required a trestle more than three, four hundred feet high—or maybe five hundred. 'If we were building her today, that's the way we'd do her.'

Once, to the southeast and east, as far as eyes could see detail, the sun was on billowing woodland; and at the horizon there were dark, indistinguishable ridges. There seemed to be no houses. One felt a thinning out of telepathic ties. Man had not yet done enough to the region to make his kind feel at home in it. Once, to the west, for a memorable second, the red sun shone full in our faces through a gaunt and abandoned old log tobacco house just above us.'

Brown, in a poetic and supercilious mood, gazed at the same view and jotted in his diary that in the meantime, 'the steward, a slender youngish man whose hair was thinning, stood at the buffet end of the car. He was neat and official in his blue suit and white vest, and looked at the floor as if nothing of grandeur were to be seen. Only occasionally did he glance up to learn if the two men were signaling for further drinks.'

The two rambled on in cumulative friendliness. One of them was interested in oil, while the other was the head of a dozen factories. They talked in millions—regardless of what they discussed. One of them said the most valued thing he possessed was his acquaintance with nice people. 'If there are any nice people in town, we know them. I wouldn't take $5 million for that—just that. Honest to God, I wouldn't.'

Soon they returned to the state of the nation. 'The real trouble with this Goddamn government,' one said finally, 'is that there's

Right: **Two young girls enjoy the amenities aboard a Southern Pacific dining car. Such service is rare today in the age of jet travel.** *Below:* **The Pennsylvania Railroad's Broad Street Station in Philadelphia.**

too much extravagance among the higher-ups.' He was now in the stage of inclusive, graceful gestures, and set out to discuss the matter in detail. But something interrupted the flow of his thought, and he ended up by insisting that he pay for the luncheon—now begun four hours ago—and for the drinks.

His friend would hear nothing of the kind. 'Or at least we'll go Dutch.' But the other was insistent, and held on to the slips which the steward had very tactfully presented face downward. He looked at the bills. Then he fumbled for his large-style reading glasses. The luncheons were $3.50; the drinks, thus far, $14.25. After swallowing once in consternation he said, 'You see, I'll just put it on my expense account.'

The other showed a ready acquiescence. 'Oh, well! That's different. If you want to let the stockholders pay it, okay, but I won't let you pay it yourself—wouldn't think of it.'

One of them begged the other to see the gorgeous sunset. It was, in Rollo Walter Brown's lexicon, not gorgeous, but, in fact, 'a washed out, pale blue-green affair hardly deserving of a glance.' But it *was* a sunset. The sun *was* going down. So the two men decided just to stay right on where they were and eat their suppers. They ordered sirloin steaks, French fried potatoes and apple pie with cheese and ice cream and coffee. An hour later, when Brown had finished his own meal and was thinking that he might go early to bed, they were having a little drink together as an aid to digestion.

The next morning Brown was awakened by 'inescapable early risers.' When he lifted the shade to see where the train was, a clear sun was coming up over low wooded mountains somewhere in eastern or southeastern Oklahoma. There were 'no accompaniments—no clouds, no mottled skies, no romantic haze; just hard outlines of gray-green flecked with settlers' unpainted low houses, and a great stark ball of deep red. I was blinded to the band of evergreen and white birches on bleak hills that stretched a thousand miles westward from New Hampshire, to the bronzing reds westward from Massachusetts and Connecticut, to the living brightness of Ohio and Indiana, to the billowing green merely touched with bright tips of red that extended from the Ozarks, back eastward across Kentucky and Virginia. Here one was in the presence of nothing but the fundamentals.'

By noon Brown stepped from the train in northern Texas, where the land bore yet another face. Cattle roamed in limitless vistas, but the trees were still green.

Right: Southern Pacific's Interurban Electric Railway carried commuters from the East Bay to San Francisco from 1936 to 1941. *Above:* A cowboy pauses amid desert splendor to watch the Southern Pacific roar by on its famed *Sunset Route.*

THE GREAT NAMES

One element of rail travel from the classic era that has been so sorely missed was that of the *named passenger route*, the *Limiteds*, the *Specials*, the *Hiawathas* and the *Zephyrs*. The very sound of these names was guaranteed to stir the imagination and titillate the hairs on the back of one's neck. These grand routes had a mystique that was reminiscent of the great ocean liners, and a magic that was never—and will never be—captured by the airlines. There was the Santa Fe's *El Capitan* that passed through the painted canyons of the great Southwest. There was the Great Northern's *Empire Builder* that took passengers from Chicago to Seattle by way of the grand scenic splendor of the northern Rockies and Glacier National Park. There was the Illinois Central's *City of New Orleans* that ran parallel to, and so perfectly captured the mood of, the great Mississippi River. There was the Canadian Pacific's *Canadian*, which defined an entire nation the way trains like the *Orange Blossom Special* and the *Coast Starlight* defined particular regions.

Glamorized trains proved spectacularly effective in the 1930s when railroad passenger traffic was in a tailspin, with trains averaging only 43 passengers per run in 1933. Then, early in 1934, came the first streamliners. Immediately, despite the Depression, these smart, fast, more comfortable trains began carrying capacity loads almost every run, and sometimes were sold out for weeks ahead. By 1939, when the average gross revenue per passenger train mile was a precarious $1.51, some streamliners were bringing in more than $5.00 per mile, and they made money for their railroads.

Of these great lines, some, such as the *Wabash Cannonball*, *Orange Blossom Special*, and *City of New Orleans*, are celebrated in song, while the *Twentieth Century Limited* became a Broadway musical thirty years after her glory days. *The Broadway Limited*, which played the nation's 'main street' in the colors of the great Pennsylvania Railroad, was also celebrated in a wonderful essay, written by Christopher Morley in 1939, that follows on page 112.

They were the 'Limiteds,' the 'Specials,' the 'Hiawathas,' the 'Zephyrs'—not to mention Rock Island's 'Rockets'—the great names of great trains that chugged west from New York and Chicago and returned from Vancouver, Seattle and San Francisco to the call of the conductor's 'All aboard!'

Below is a partial list of North America's greatest routes and the names they bore.

Abraham Lincoln
  Chicago—St Louis
Adirondack
  Montreal—New York
Arrowhead
  Duluth—Minneapolis
Banker's
  Springfield—Washington
Bar Harbor Express
  Bar Harbor—Washington
Bear Mountain
  Albany—New York
Benjamin Franklin
  Boston—Philadelphia

Betsy Ross
  New York—Washington
Birmingham Special
  New York—Birmingham
Black Hawk
  Los Angeles—Dubuque
Blue Ridge
  Martinsburg—Washington
Blue Water Limited
  Chicago—Port Huron
Bostonian
  Boston—New York
Broadway Limited
  New York—Chicago

California Zephyr
  Chicago—Los Angeles
Canadian
  Montreal—Vancouver
Cascade Daylight
  Portland—San Francisco
Century
  Chicago—Los Angeles
Champion
  New York—St Petersburg
Chief
  Chicago—Los Angeles
Choctaw Rocket
  Memphis—Oklahoma City
Clamdigger
  Providence—New Haven
City of Denver
  Chicago—Denver
City of Los Angeles
  Chicago—Los Angeles
City of New Orleans
  Chicago—New Orleans

City of Portland
  Chicago—Portland
City of San Francisco
  Chicago—San Francisco
Coast Daylight
  Seattle—Los Angeles
Coast Starlight
  Seattle—Los Angeles
Colonial
  Boston—Newport News
Congressional
  New York—Washington
Corn Belt Rocket
  Chicago—Omaha
Des Moines Rocket
  Chicago—Des Moines
Detroit Arrow
  Chicago—Detroit
DeWitt Clinton
  Albany—New York
El Capitan
  Chicago—Los Angeles

Below: Southern Pacific's famed *Coast Daylight*.

Embassy
New York—Washington
Empire Builder
Chicago—Seattle
Empire State Express
New York—Cleveland
FFV
New York—Cincinnati
Federal
Boston—Washington
Florida Arrow
Chicago—Miami
Florida Special
New York—Miami
Floridian
Chicago—Miami
Flying Yankee
Boston—Philadelphia
Golden State
Chicago—Los Angeles
Havana Special
New York—Key West
Henry Hudson
Albany—New York
Hilltopper
Washington—Chicago
Illini
Chicago—Urbana
Illinois Zephyr
Chicago—Quincy
Imperial
Chicago—Los Angeles
Inter American
Chicago—Laredo
James Whitcomb Riley
Washington—Chicago
Jeffersonian
New York—St Louis
John Adams
Boston—Philadelphia
Lake Shore Limited
New York—Buffalo
Lark
San Francisco—Los Angeles
Lone Star
Chicago—Houston

Merchant's
Boston—Washington
Miamian
New York—Miami
Michigan Executive
Detroit—Jackson
Mid City Express
Chicago—Detroit
Minute Man
Boston—Washington
Montrealer
Montreal—New York
Murray Hill
New York—Washington
National Dream
Calgary—Vancouver
National Limited
New York—Chicago
Niagara Rainbow
New York—Detroit
Night Owl
Boston—Washington
North Coast Hiawatha
Chicago—Seattle
North Coast Limited
Chicago—Seattle
Olympian Hiawatha
Chicago—Seattle
Orange Blossom Special
Boston—Miami
Overland
Chicago—San Francisco
Pacific International
Seattle—Vancouver
Palmetto
New York—Savannah
Palmland
New York—Miami
Panama Limited
Chicago—New Orleans
Patriot
Boston—Washington
Peoria Rocket
Chicago—Peoria
Piedmont Limited
New York—New Orleans

Pilgrim
Boston—Philadelphia
Pioneer
Salt Lake City—Seattle
Pioneer Zephyr
Chicago—Denver
Quad City Rocket
Chicago—Rock Island
Quaker
Boston—Philadelphia
Red Bird
Chicago—Detroit
Rio Grande Zephyr
Denver—Salt Lake City
Rocky Mountain Rocket
Chicago—Colorado Springs
Royal Gorge
Denver—Salt Lake City
Saint Clair
Detroit—Chicago
Salt City Express
New York—Syracuse
San Diegans
Los Angeles—San Diego
San Francisco Zephyr
Chicago—San Francisco
San Joaquin
San Francisco—Bakersfield
Senator
Boston—Washington
Shasta Daylight
Portland—San Francisco
Shawnee
Chicago—Carbondale
Shenandoah
Washington—Cincinnati
Silver Meteor
New York—Miami
Silver Star
New York—St Petersburg
South Wind
Chicago—Miami
Southern Crescent
New York—New Orleans
Southern Railway Express
New York—Atlanta

Southerner
New York—New Orleans
Southland
Chicago—Miami
Southwest Limited
Chicago—Los Angeles
State House
Chicago—St Louis
Sun Queen
New York—Miami
Sunbeam
Dallas—Houston
Sundown
Boston—New York
Sunset Limited
New Orleans—Los Angeles
Sunshine Special
New York—Texas
Super Chief
Chicago—Los Angeles
Super Continental
Montreal—Vancouver
Twentieth Century Limited
New York—Chicago
Twilight Limited
Detroit—Chicago
Twin Star Rocket
Minneapolis—Houston
Vacationer
New York—Miami
Valley Forge
New York—Harrisburg
Washington Irving
Albany—New York
Water Level Express
New York—Buffalo
Western Star
Chicago—Seattle
William Penn
Boston—Philadelphia
Wolverine
Detroit—Chicago
Zephyr Rocket
Minneapolis—St Louis

ON THE BROADWAY LIMITED

The long windows were clear and luxurious above the shadowy platform (Union Station in Chicago). In the observation car and in armchairs and staterooms people were already at ease—comfortable people in the peace of Sunday afternoon—confiding people, who take things for granted. Secretly, even humbly, I felt my difference. Promoted for the moment from passenger to crew, I was putting on complicated overalls under the tuition of Mr Burchiel, road foreman of engines. Like a god, even my life was not my own. I had signed for the Pennsylvania Railroad an extensive document, renouncing, for unwitting heirs, executors, assigns, publishers, attorneys and innkeepers, any peevishness they might feel if things went wrong.

The Pennsy's locomotive number 5493 was waiting. I looked at her with the uncomprehending adoration one feels for locomotives; beside whom, since they have grown in the same scale as ourselves, every man is still a small boy. She was monstrous and cast a darkness about her in the dull November light. She had lately come from the rebuilding shops, where they gave her an enormous net tender, a huge, black, shiny tank, smooth and flush. 'Not a rivet in it,' said Mr Burchiel proudly. Her driving

wheels stood as solid as the foundations of a church. (I wish Euclid could have seen them.)

It's not possible, the mind said, that such weights can be moved. Yet it is done, by the dynamics of hatred. Here are a tank of inert water, a box of angry fire. They damn each other by instinct, cat and dog. Of their indignation, hiss and growl and spit, those wheels make 90 miles an hour.

There was, however, no time for moralizing, even the most naive. Mr Burchiel and I climbed into the cab, where Mike Bruicks, the engineer, and Louis Koch, the fireman, were ready. It is Mr Burchiel's job to supervise the actual operation of locomotives in that division, but with two old-timers like Bruicks (43 years in service) and Koch (30 years) it is companionship rather than checkup.

Mike was on his padded bench, with the forward gaze that an engineer has which never varies. You wonder, after watching for a couple of hours, if he can look sideways. He'll shout you an occasional remark, but his eyes don't leave the track. Louis was studying his fire. He trod a foot pedal which split the up and down doors. Locomotive 5493 has automatic stoking. The coal, crushed small, feeds up into the furnace through a worm onto a

The Pennsylvania Railroad's *Broadway Limited*, one of the finest passenger trains of its day, raced from New York to Chicago in record time. Fire and water and the power of a 4-6-2 Pacific locomotive *(below)* made those wheels turn at an incredible 90 miles an hour. Pennsy also used 2-8-2 Mikado locomotives (like the one *above*).

flat plate, where jets of steam spray it to all parts of the fire. It looked to be a pretty complete combustion to me, but Louis was not satisfied. We all had a drink of very cold water from the spout of a can, and while I was still wondering where to stow myself, we were off. 'Highball' (not like the drink, but both words accented equally), Louis shouted as each signal bridge came in view. Mike, on the other side of the cab, tallied it by repeating.

There was just room for me to perch on the forward end of Louis's bench. The main steampipe, which heats the whole train, toasted my knee. Two lighted lanterns were at my feet, and I could see the track ahead. I'm afraid I tried to look as professional as possible, so as not to give anything away, but I was in a haze. A great black slope of dials, gauges, handles; a blur of hissing, piping and rumbling clatter; a desire not to be in the way, is all I remember for the first few minutes.

'There's the *Central Flyer*,' said Louis as we pulled into Englewood, seven miles from Union Station. She's due to leave just as we get in.'

The steam turbine engine used turbine blades, not pistons, to turn the wheels. This powerful locomotive (*below*) weighed over one million pounds.

It was our great rival, the *Twentieth Century*, in whose cab I had once ridden. Yes, she was just pulling out. From the cab of the New York Central's locomotive 5318, her engineer waved me a gesture of admiration for our new tender, much bigger than his own. Twenty-five tons of coal and 35,000 gallons of water that tender carries, and 5318 was evidently envious. I waved back, conveying (I hope) that that's the sort of thing we're used to on the Pennsy. I saw *Van Twiller*, *Star Light* (individual cars, as well as entire trains, had given names) and other cars rumble by. Our own *Herald Square*, *Craigie House*, *James Whitcomb Riley*, etc —would get to Penn Station tomorrow morning at the same moment that the others were slowing into Grand Central.

'Water Level Route?' later said Mr Grady, the train secretary. 'Sure, it's a good slogan, but they have to go 60 miles farther than we do.' After Englewood, Louis began overhauling the fire. He was breaking up great clogs of soft gold with a long hook. He got the feed valve adjusted to his pleasure. 'Clear' was now his shout, instead of 'Highball.' He was courteous to yell in my ear everything he thought I ought to know; but as the noise increased I'm afraid I missed some of it. For, as she began to show what was in her, she opened a vast, roaring undersong, strangely like the yell of a thousand bagpipes. The long, musical

blast of the whistle was almost continuous; the traditional two longs, a short, a very long. Raving imperative in the first bellow (defiance, warning, blasphemy complete; the bearded damnation of a god in righteous fury) then dying away, in the final wail, to deep-chested sorrow for all the fools of the world. You saw them skipping across the track at suburban stations, or wondering whether they could make it at an unguarded country crossing.

Mike let me take a hand at the cord. 'The point is,' he remarked crisply, 'to keep blowing right up to the crossing.'

'You'll see some of the things we have to worry about,' said Mr Burchiel, who was keeping an eye on everything. 'Some of these automobile trucks are getting big enough so you know it when you hit them.'

Almost at that moment Louis, who was on the other side of the cab, gave a yell. It was too late for me to see—we had gone 1000 feet before I could stumble over—but he told me that a car, trying to beat the train, had pulled up about three feet away from us. It was Sunday dusk; there were many cars on the roads, all pushing home for supper. I hope that the unknown citizen of Indiana ate his with a thoughtful heart. As for me, I've stuck my nose into the gale as the *Broadway Limited* roared over several

hundred crossings. If they'd take my word for it, she can't dodge, and there'd never be another Sunday night supper congealing uneaten.

Somewhere beyond Gary we got an *Approach*—three lights in diagonal instead of vertical, which means reduce speed, with possible stop on the next two-mile block. I believe it was the Grand Trunk line which had to be crossed. The next signal was 'Clear' and we picked up speed again, but it had cost us two or three minutes. In a schedule which allows 16.5 hours for 908 miles, every hour must count for over 55 miles, every minute lost puts one a mile behind.

Now, as the brown prairie faded into dusk, Mike began to let her travel. Leaning out beyond the narrow glass screen I could just glimpse the great knuckled cranks flying like horse's hoofs. Her huge black shape, stretching high before us, was too big to see in full. Louis's shout of 'Clear' at every two-mile signal had a note of exultation. The great pile of coal behind us sank visibly. In the vibration a good deal would jostle down onto the steel floor, and every now and then Louis would shovel it up, a long throw (higher than his head) back into the tender.

'A hell of a way to fire an engine,' he said jocularly—'backwards.'

A man who has fired an engine by hand speaks of the automatic method as a writer speaks of Kipling or Chaucer. You should hear Louis pay homage to the Standard Stoker. In his days of hand firing he 'shoveled enough coal to cover the whole United States feet deep.'

Now we were coming to the upgrade towards Valparaiso. 'But it's all upgrade when you're firing by hand. Want to see some pink ice cream?' he says, and opens the fire doors.

The furnace, big as a bungalow, is a naked vault of flame, the brick lining seems actually soft and lathery with molten blaze, an absolute essence of fire, white below, and rose above. A terrifying sight, from which you recoil in dismay. 'Pretty good,' says Louis; and Mr Burchiel's comment is, 'That's perfection.'

In such a furnace there is no bed of coals; the fuel is deified before it ever touches bottom.

We roared through Valparaiso, a white island of snow in the dun twilight. That town, Louis tells me, gets snow earlier and keeps it longer than any other in the state, and no one knows why.

There's another upgrade towards Plymouth; we frolic it at 75 mph.

It's growing dark. A broad band of light spreads before us. A locomotive, like a motor car, dims its lamp as it approaches another train, so as not to dazzle the engineer. Louis, squatting behind, takes just as good care of me as if I'd never signed that release. He knows every curve by heart (there *are* some, even though it looks so straight on the map), and if I happen to be standing up gazing stupidly about he warns me to hang on. When we meet another train he pulls me away from the window. Sometimes something sticks out or flies off. The grade near Plymouth is called Over the Hill to the Poorhouse! There actually *is* a poorhouse. Louis points it out as we yell by. 'Where all the railroad men go when they get through.'

Over the hill we really shove. I see Mike scooping out his watch. I find mine too, fumbling under flaps of overall. We're going to be a couple of minutes late? Louis denies it. 'Mike and I are never late. We get there on time if we tear the wheels off her. She has what it takes.'

She has indeed. 'Clear… Clear…'

Even that routine cry, in Louis's Indiana tenor, sounds a tone of mystic fervor, orgiastic surrender. As far as I'm concerned, reason is gone; this is religion. Against the fan of lift her great bulk looms monstrous, a raving meteor of sound and mass. 'He's giving it to her,' Louis screams.

'How fast?' I yell. 'About ninety.'

The sliding window creeps back in the wind pressure, the lighted lanterns dance over my feet… all the world's bagpipes sing, the airbrake valve chirps like a bird in a cage… Mike's eyes are ahead, his hand forever on the brake. The mind can't think forward or back, is fulfilled with Now. I cannot analyze, this is mere ecstasy, madness under control, like writing *Moby Dick*.

Mr Burchiel, satisfied and watchful, pulls out on the hose and wets down the coal in the tender. I even see him, over by the canvas curtain that flaps in a hurricane, take the water can and swig a drink. There are lights of cars along the road. Through towns and stations we rip, tearing a strip of muslin; but there are no likes for this. Villages are torn open, blotted out by our frightful howl. They are wiped away, blown behind us.

Louis turns the feed valve a trifle. Soot is gritting under my goggles. 'Clear… Clear…'

Whistle stops like this one in Wawa, Pennsylvania *(left)* once dotted the United States. Here a Pennsy train makes a brief stop on a sunny March day. Though the trees are still bare, the workers' light clothing tells us that spring will soon return to the Pennsylvania countryside.

When the whistle yells, we fly through a fog of steam, blinded for the moment by our own safety cry.

Keep—out—of—my—wa-a-a-a-y.

I lean out as far as I dare. We take a curve that surprises me. It doesn't seem to bother her.

'Yes,' says Louis, 'she's an easy riding engine.'

The lights of Fort Wayne appear. This is the division town, home of Mike and Louis and many other railroad men. The locomotive called 5493 will go on to Crestline, but Mike and Louis will stop here, and bring Number 28 back to Chicago at 4:55 tomorrow morning. Incidentally, they don't speak of the *Broadway Limited*. That's passenger and publicity talk. To them, she's Number 28.

I think the only serious error I made was in saying 'What's the population of Fort Wayne? About 50,000?'

Louis was outraged. 'My God, we've got 120,000, and one of the finest courthouses you ever set foot in.'

Fort Wayne... 148 miles in 140 minutes, including a stop at Englewood, and the first 20 miles through crowded tracks. Just time to shake hands and wriggle out of overalls. 'Better get on in front and walk through,' said the conductor, 'we're pulling out.' He suggested that I clean up at the first washroom, but I insisted on walking all the way back to the passenger car, *Herald Square*. I wanted Colatine to see my face.

Extraordinary how quiet it was back in that drawing room (the next-to-last car). Even though I knew 5493 was again doing a comfortable 70 mph, you'd think we were scarcely moving. Till we went forward to the diner, we couldn't even hear her whistle.

I woke, as I always do by instinct, just where I would have wished, at the Horseshoe Curve. The night had cleared, there was a wide lace of stars, and Orion watching the track of the Milky Way.

At Altoona at 3 am, locomotives were standing in sociable groups in the dark; white aigrettes of steam were rising into the stillness, somehow like Queen Mary's hat. On the next track was a long string of silent cars, the maroon and gold of my first love, and a figure standing watchful with a lantern at the tail end, faithful as Orion. He was doing his job, and I rendered him a private, unsuspected homage.

Again, a little after seven, I looked out as we flashed in sunrise, swiftly by familiar names. Strafford, Wayne, St Davids, Radnor, Villanova, Rosemont, Bryn Mawr, Haverford. Then I remembered. When I was a boy at college I lived three years in a dormitory not far from the Pennsylvania Railroad's Main Line. My bedroom window was toward the tracks, and twice a day a certain train caught my ear. About 7:15 in the morning it came rocketing down from the West, making a final sprint for Philadelphia. That was time to get up. There was just enough warning for the bath and the half-mile walk to breakfast. And about 7:15 in the evening, a strong, difficult, puffing upgrade, outward bound for names of mystery—incredibly remote—Harrisburg, Pittsburgh and Chicago. That was just after supper, and it meant time to sit down under the green glass lampshade and get to work. Vaguely, as one turned to physics or French or Chaucer, that heavy rolling passage was both sedative and spur. It meant fidelity to task, and yet also escape into fancy. Ohio, Indiana, Illinois; the Alleghanies, the Horseshoe Curve, the Johnstown Flood; all these were in that receding sound, with click and tremor of the rails narrowing in moonlight towards Bryn Mawr.

That train was, and still is, the *Broadway Limited*.

—Christopher Morley (1939)

As the 1930s drew to a close, electric trains were introduced. *Below:* Commuters gather around *The Metropolitan* on a brisk January day in 1938. It was the first electric train in Harrisburg, Pennsylvania.

TWILIGHT ON THE CITY OF SAN FRANCISCO

It was the last year of world peace before the cataclysm, that year of 1939. It was the end of so many eras, and it was the year in which we have chosen to visit the *Broadway Limited* and the *City of San Francisco*. For the former, it was a celebration of power that symbolized 40 years about to end, while for the latter, it was metaphoric of the twilight in that golden age of rail travel.

Among the great 'named routes' few were so powerful, and so pretentious in their wielding of that power, than the *City of San Francisco*, an enormous, gleaming zephyr that ran between Chicago and its namesake by the Golden Gate. The *City of San Francisco* was such a haughty grande dame that she was too massive for one railroad to handle. The Southern Pacific, the Union Pacific and the Milwaukee Road all played a role in pulling her for part of her journey.

She was to the rails what the *Titanic* had been to the waves: the largest, most beautiful, fastest, most elegant and modern of machinery in a century just into its second generation of idolizing such technology. And like the *Titanic*, she was considered 'indestructible.'

She represented not the overstuffed velvet, carved ivory and inlaid wood luxury of the grand Victorian and Edwardian steam trains, but the flawless fit of form to function of sleek cocktail gowns in an Art Deco lounge. Fred Astaire could have danced through her tavern car on its semi-circular, chrome-trimmed tables over crescent leather booths—Bauhaus in motion. Her power units, comprising the longest locomotive ever built, consisted of six 900 horsepower, 12 cylinder diesels, the most powerful in the world, capable of hurtling 600 tons of silver voracity at speeds reaching 110 miles per hour. She made the trip from Chicago to San Francisco in what then defined style. Her cars bore the names of famed San Francisco locales: *Market Street* and *Portsmouth Square*, *Seal Rock*, *Chinatown* and *Twin Peaks*, the *Presidio*, *Telegraph Hill*, *Union Square*, and *Mission Dolores*.

Passengers could take a drink at the *Nob Hill* amid the soft glow of blonde brass fixtures; put their dry martinis down on circular, mirrored cocktail tables at the *Embarcadero*. Later, they could recline among smoke grays, beige tans, French greens, Nantes blue, apricot and jonquil interiors, or sit in the observation car, the longest passenger car in the world, and watch where they had just been rushed to get out of the way of where they were going. The light was glareless. The air was conditioned. The 39 hour trip, only one full night, was just a bit shorter than the virtue of most women of that generation. Otherwise it was paradise.

The cheapest ticket was five dollars; the most expensive, at 22, booked a suite that slept four and had its own sofa and bathroom. Three squares ran 90 cents a day in 1939, and that included a three-course meal that most women probably wouldn't have been able to finish. If one wanted to listen to the radio, it was anywhere on the train. One could pick up a phone and call the staff at any time. At main passenger terminals, one could pick up the same phone and call Tokyo. If you had a headache, you wouldn't have needed to worry, as the stewardesses were all registered nurses. The scenery was indescribably beautiful, and that which kept you from it was a car twice the tensile strength of steel.

The *Titanic* of the rails, indeed, and on the night of 12 August 1939, she was heading for a disaster far more deplorable because it lacked the indifference and majesty—the moral unimpeachability—of an archipelago of ice (a collision with which, after all, could have been avoided). No, what sank the *City of San Francisco* was no ice-island of bad luck, but four and a half inches of craven and crazed malice which went unforeseen, and only God could have circumvented.

At 9:35 am on 11 August, it was already 95 degrees at 90 percent humidity in Chicago, and the city's profile, draped in a reddish haze, was about as low as a side of beef. The only thing running more regularly than the trains was mascara. Dresses clung, children shrieked and Hawaiian shirts seemed ready to blossom into full and fragrant bloom. Tenement after tenement of dilapidation, factories, slaughterhouses, and cattle barns sweltered, and the slow, thick Chicago river—like the marrow of the town—rolled past their windows. A billboard giant advertising cigarettes blew smoke rings down Wabash Avenue, like infernal halos looking for a saint.

The *City of San Francisco* waited at the biggest train station on the continent. It was 800 feet long, 400 feet wide, with a main concourse ceilinged at 165 feet, forested with fluted columns that stood against frosted glass panes which reflected a Tennessee marble floor space capable of holding 38,000. Alive with humanity and newspapers, Union Station held more electric fans than orchids in a nursery greenhouse. Everyone looked impatient to be somewhere else, and a little sick to be there.

'Railroading is a thankless job,' said an old engineer to Ed Hecox, engineer of the *City of San Francisco*. 'Bad work, bad weather and bad hours. If I were a young man again, I'd never go near a locomotive. There was a time when one man was a little better'n another, and the good man got the good engine and the good job and kept 'em both. Nowadays, a man is just a little interchangeable piece of machine, works when and where they tell him to, and sleeps when he gets a chance. No credit for what he does right, but the minute he slips up a little, the office hollers, "Thirty days." '

The old engineer was 74 and the Southern Pacific had kept him for more than thirty of those years.

Right: **The *City of San Francisco* at the Oakland Pier in 1938. This Queen of the Rails ran from Chicago to San Francisco—across the plains, over the mountains—decked out in shiny chrome and brass fixtures, smooth leather booths and mirrored tables. Once the only way to travel across the country, she has sadly been replaced by a more expeditious, though less gracious, form of travel—the jetliner.**

By 9:55 the *City of San Francisco* was backing onto the passenger platform amid the usual inchoate murmurs of approval and wonder. A fresh blue-gray uniform sitting smartly on an even fresher-looking stewardess, who leaned out and announced, 'Welcome aboard.' A caterpillar of bobbing basket lunches, fluttering fans, draped jackets like rotten fruit, the mysterious emanations of this season's hat, glistening flesh and the little flecks of redcap, all stirred before the immaculate silver, shimmering shell of the train. With a last shudder of expectation, the human caterpillar dispersed into the metal one. At 10:02—seven minutes behind schedule—the *City of San Francisco* was on its way, crawling past the stockyards, and soon the farmlands, the trees like starving mendicants, the cattle like flies on a card table, the slowly evaporating Great Plains. On toward the immense, the truly immense, sky it slid, and everything else slid behind.

One will sleep and wake when one is hungry. The ground is moving at 84 miles per hour underneath and there's no question of drawing blood as a stewardess holds an open straight razor steadily over the lathered face of a paralytic.

Between sleep and consciousness, one sleeping on a train falls into the usually suppressed universe of sound. With no cross-chatter from the other senses, without the obsession with limit and definition that vision imposes, the aural cosmos offers the more immediate sensation of timelessness and hallucination—such a sensation, perhaps, as one comes to before almost waking to what sounds like the climax of a wild Wagnerian drama: a sustained high note of unbearable intensity and inhuman constancy; duration and violence seems to be cutting through a deafening background of rhythmic roar. It's been there all along. When one opens one's eyes, it recedes into intelligibility—the sound of a high speed rail from the inside!

A passenger raised the shades, and suddenly there was a hops field in Missouri. 'You could use a beer,' he said to himself as he rose to take a small walk past America to the diner. 'What a crop of faces the country grows,' he observed as he sought to take the reserve out of his own. Train travel liberates the garrulous and secures them an opportunity to our affections.

In the club car, the air smelled faintly of bay rum and lavender, and it was 68 degrees—all the time. In the diner it got warmer, and as one walked through, one would notice that the hurriedly eating porters have been in full sweat for some time. They smiled as the head steward approached with a certain supercilious affability and unctuousness. 'They tip on this train—and well,' thought the traveler. A BLT and a beer is little enough to divert him from the scenery, which is suddenly in a downpour.

He remembers that, as they say in the Midwest, 'If you don't like the weather, wait a minute and it'll change.' He blinked and turned to find that someone slim, bright and female was sitting across from him. Having exchanged polite destinations with the young lady, he glanced at the head steward, reflecting that 'They know *how* to earn their tips on this train.'

It was hot enough to bake bread! Thunder and lightning. Everyone looked out the window at once as the silence lengthened. The engineer up front lit his pipe, as the darkness descended a little early. The languor of the countryside beneath the lowering sky, the rise and fall of other's voices, the opportunities for self-display and engaging others, as well as poker. *Vanity Fair*, letter writing, brandy and the ball game passed the time. Nebraska, Colorado, Utah, oats, oleander and arroyos, and

Left: **The *City of San Francisco* was once the longest, fastest, most beautiful and most elegant train to grace the rails. So grand was she that she needed more than one railroad to handle her and was jointly operated by the Southern Pacific, Union Pacific and Chicago & NorthWestern.**

then a stop for an hour at Salt Lake City before the ride over the mountain-framed inland sea of the lake. Beyond, the desert sun is like a fire, lounging over a salt-caked pan. Late in the afternoon on 12 August 1939, Montello, Cobre, Deeth and Halleck had passed, as had Elko and Carlin, and the train stopped at

Below: **Shiny and sleek, the *City of San Francisco* readies herself at Chicago's Union Station for her cross-country journey.**

Palisades. The passengers watched the moon sit above the spectacular cliffs that gave the town its name. 'What do people do out here anyway?,' someone asked, cognizant of the one-room shack where a still employed man lives, but oblivious to the new irrigation unit outside of town. It was another space, another time, even though the shack was full of magazines discarded from the *City of San Francisco*.

Nearly two decades earlier, in October 1919, the Southern

Pacific police force, then the largest private police force in the world, had to remove 20,643 'undesirable persons' from the railroad's property. This was before the Depression, and things didn't get any easier then. In the first seven months of 1939, over 700 people quit or had to be laid off in the Salt Lake City division alone. In another space, another time, Hitler was demanding Danzig, but on this continent, there were two World's Fairs going on simultaneously.

The view from where the traveler sat atop Ten Mile Canyon was breathtaking. The stars had never seemed so bright before. At Harney, a single passenger boards for what will be the shortest train trip of his life.

'O dark dark dark. They all go into the dark,
The vacant interstellar spaces, the vacant into the vacant,
The captains, merchant bankers, eminent men of letters,
The generous patrons of art, the statesmen and the ruler,
Distinguished civil servants, chairmen of many committees,
Industrial lords and petty contractors, all go into the dark.'

On the night of 12 August 1939, at a place known as nothing more than Bridge Four, a mile and a half out of Harney, the *City of San Francisco* derails. The five middle cars—the diners *Presidio* and *Mission Dolores*—and the three sleepers—*Embarcadero*, *Twin Peaks*, and *Chinatown*—pulverized the bridge and slammed into the small canyon below with all the force that 5400 horsepower powering 600 tons at 60 mph could give them. They wound up looking like nothing so much as a bunch of silver cigar tubes a goat had mangled and left in a ditch. All the luxurious fittings became so much deadly shrapnel, and cars, caskets for 24 people. There is almost nothing left of the *Presidio*, in which 18 alone died, the other cars having slammed into it and cut it in half. The three power units, following the guardrails of the bridge, miraculously crossed it and pulled two cars across with them. The engineer, having applied the emergency brake at almost precisely the moment of derailment, saved the remaining seven cars from plunging into the canyon, although *Fisherman's Wharf* was hanging out over the practically dry Humboldt River like an amputated arm.

There was the silence of the desert night for a moment before the cries of pain set in. Someone saw an earless man scamper away from a vantage point. What could a saboteur looking down on that scene have thought? Might he have wondered why they always call trains 'she'? Today—indeed even a half century ago—it would be hopeless to speculate on such things because it is impossible to know him. He proved to be more immaterial than the night itself.

The Southern Pacific subsequently launched the biggest private manhunt in history, and in the 12 years that followed the accident, Chief Special Agent Dan O'Connell interviewed over 12,000 persons and handled 200,000 pieces of evidence. Nothing tangible was ever produced on a possible saboteur. Evidence was found indicating that the south rail, a short distance before the bridge and on the outside of the three degree turn, had been shifted inward 4.5 inches. To this day, there is a $10,000 reward for information leading to an arrest and conviction.

The *City of San Francisco* continued to make her run—to the San Francisco World's Fair of 1939-1940—and all through the war years. In 1952 she became snowbound on Donner Pass (*see pp 170–171*) on the California side of the Sierra Nevada, but there was general cozy frivolity and no loss of life.

Ultimately, however, the grande dame began to grow dowdy, and those who would have once made the trip no other way, now took an airplane.

THE GOLDEN TWILIGHT

1940-1955

PART THREE

THE GOLDEN TWILIGHT

By Bill Yenne

T he golden age of American rail travel probably ended with World War II. One can say 'with' because it really happened neither before or after.

For the railroad companies themselves, the war years were boom years for their passenger business. Hundreds of thousands of young men, who would never have traveled by train (or perhaps *at all*), were simultaneously drafted and had to be

Below and opposite: **During wartime, trains were packed with sailors and soldiers off to boot camp.**

transported from their homes to Army camps thousands of miles away. Meanwhile, people who in peacetime would have driven their automobiles were forced onto the passenger trains by gasoline rationing.

Unfortunately, to accommodate this huge increase in ridership, there was nowhere near a proportional increase in the number of available passenger cars. With wartime shortages, extra rail cars couldn't have been built even if the railroad companies would have *wanted* to build them. Thus, for the American rail passenger, World War II was no golden era.

'Long, long ago, at least three years back,' wrote Lucy Greenbaum in 1943, 'when a speculative soul rode on a peacetime train, it was possible for him to enjoy the quiet, leisurely trip. He could muse about life in the abstract. Inspired by the scenic beauty whizzing past at 60 mph, his thoughts could range the universe. As the spinning wheels hummed out the song of time through space there came the chance to relax. No offender could blow smoke around except in the club car or diner. Conversation buzzed in low, confidential tones so that gently nodding businessmen and sweet old ladies could sleep undisturbed. Topics varied from the scenery to the weather to the chances of the next Republican candidate winning the Presidency. The world's woes rested only in skeleton weight on individual shoulders.'

Ms Greenbaum recalled that passengers even laughed tolerantly when a baby's bawling split the air. Old folks traveled for pleasure, young ones for a lark. Friendly foursomes found time for bridge. Anyone who wanted a meal wandered into the diner, chatted with the steward, lazily ordered and ate. The pounding of the wheels took precedence over all other noise. 'One was conscious first of the train as an instrument of transportation,' she recalled, 'then, secondly, of the assortment of fellow travelers that happened to be aboard.'

'But no more,' mused Ms Greenbaum in 1943. The tempo had changed from 'the slow, calm rhythm of a Strauss waltz to the hot, dashing beat of a Jersey Bounce. Noise circles around, drops low, hums up again, but never retreats. The off-beat of the train wheels is drowned in a solid stream of chatter... There is just room enough in which to laugh. Any gesture of annoyance or sign of irritation would mean displacement. No one could afford that. Or the greater evil: to be thought of by the other passengers as a poor sport, the worst thing any American can be called.'

The detail with which Lucy Greenbaum described the heretofore gentile sojourn from Boston to New York is at once delightful in its humor and profound in its lasting historical importance as a first person account of rail travel in 1943.

BOSTON TO NEW YORK IN WARTIME

People stood jammed together, staring at the closed gates with such fiery intensity that they seemed to be waiting for St Peter. But it turned out to be only the six o'clock train to New York.

Sprawling South Station in Boston surged with the moving feet of rushing humanity. The information booth was buried under hordes of the puzzled and the lost. Impatient civilians stood listening to servicemen's 'information pleas' — 'How do Ah git to Nawfolk?' 'Could you tell me how to hit Chicago?' Located practically mid-station, a liquor store carried on a roaring business. Concessions sold candy like hotcakes. Magazines and newspaper piles steadily cascaded lower and lower. Soldiers and sailors, especially the bulbous ones, leaned against food counters, stuffing themselves with hot dogs and ice cream.

'Train to Providence, New London, New Haven and New York,' droned a trainman. Like a football team, the crowd caught the signal. Long, tender looks between couples changed into hasty kisses. People swooped down on their bags, hurled themselves forward.

Crowds catapulted me through the gates. I floated along the train shed, borne by a Wave and two apprentice seamen. We sailed past coach after coach, finally broke through the barrage to stagger up the steps of an already crammed car. Passengers had plumped themselves down on all available brown plush. Only the narrow aisle stretched before us, cold and hard.

I rode on a suitcase from Boston to New York. If I hadn't been lucky enough to bring luggage I would have traveled the 230 miles on my high-heeled shoes. As crowded as a subway at rush hour is no longer a strong simile. Not in wartime. The upper level of travel is holding more than its own.

Boston, cradle of American liberty and home of the baked bean, soon became merely a memory. Scenes soaked in American history faded into the now familiar faces of fellow travelers. A stolid man rose to plow into the men's room. Two middle-aged ladies timidly tripped their way toward the diner.

With the bravado of commandos, several children swaggered along, clutching comic books as weapons of aggression. Children add to the general confusion, divide the quiet in half, multiply the annoyances and should be subtracted during wartime travel. Even intrepid soldiers cower before cuties. Many of them, however, are sons and daughters of fighting men, en route to a port city to visit daddy, and so must be forgiven their small sins.

The car door opened. The conductor stuck his head inside as far as he could without appearing to kiss a middle-aged lady standing in the aisle:

'New London!' he yelled.

A flurry followed. Some sailors prepared to disembark. Standees with strength left stood poised to dive into the nearest seat the second it was vacated. However, they got small chance. A few seamen dropped off but hundreds spilled on. Ensigns from the Coast Guard Academy, Merchant Mariners from Fort Trumbull, soldiers from Fort Wright, war workers from nearby plants, sailors from Avery Point and the submarine base, joined the crew from Boston.

As they plummeted through the door I found myself carried into the lap of a young, handsome sailor.

'Have a cigarette,' he offered with the aplomb of most Navy men. Realizing it would require a herculean maneuver to reach into his pocket, he amended, 'Let's go into the diner and have a drink.'

He played interference and I squeezed in the openings. We slugged our way through two cars and were brought to a halt by a gang in search of sustenance. While we waited there was the chance to exchange life histories. He was an aerial photographer for the Navy and expected to spend most of his furlough on roller skates.

'Brought 'em down with me,' he explained. 'That's why my suitcase weighs a ton.'

He was disappointed because he was the only one of his gang still in this country. The rest were scattered worldwide. 'I guess it's natural to fight,' he mused. 'At the base the guys are either fighting the Civil War all over again or arguing whether Philly or Pittsburgh's a better city.'

Over a Scotch and soda he confessed that he had run away from home when he was 15. His family were Quakers and could not understand why he would join the Navy.

'I'm the black sheep of the family,' he announced proudly.

The train swept into the night. The whitecaps of Long Island Sound became blacked out as shades were drawn. Sailors and soldiers started to wilt into sleep. It was as though some unseen enemy had raced through and hammered them all over the head.

Soldiers stretched out, legs and arms flung wildly at all angles. Sailors sleep differently. While the soldier man lounges in wide latitude, the sailor tar curls up into a tight ball. He

There's room for both...IF !

As THINGS NOW STAND, there are enough Pullman cars to meet all requirements for troop transportation without seriously affecting civilian passenger service IF . . .

civilian travelers cooperate in making capacity use of cars!

Therefore, you *help your own cause* by following these simple suggestions whenever you make an overnight trip:

1. *Make reservations as early as possible.* This gives Pullman time to send cars *where* they are needed *when* they are needed.

2. *Cancel reservations promptly if plans change.* This avoids wasteful vacancies by making available to others the space being held for you.

3. *Ask your ticket salesman on which days Pullmans are least crowded and try to travel on those days.* This helps spread travel evenly throughout the week.

4. *Take as little luggage as you can.* This gives you and your fellow passengers more room to relax in the car.

It is definitely encouraging that very few people, so far, have failed to obtain Pullman accommodations on the trains they have wanted to take, even though civilian travel has increased and so many sleeping cars are needed to move troops.

In some cases, of course, passengers don't get the exact *type* of accommodation they ask for. But whether you sleep in an upper, a lower, a section or a room, you enjoy the comfortable privacy of a soft, full-sized Pullman bed.

And you get the "*sleep* going" that is so important when you have to "*keep* going" at an all-out wartime pace.

SLEEP GOING—
To KEEP GOING—
Go Pullman

Copyright 1942, The Pullman Co.

squeezes into the most cramped positions, arms tight against his sides, legs tucked up under him.

It was the sailors who rolled upon the floors, coats as pillows, caps shading their eyes. They have even removed baggage from the overhead racks and nestled up there.

The ticket collector does not disturb the sleep of fighting men. He plucks tickets from out of shoes, from behind ears, from hats.

Law and order officially ride the rails in the club cars—these new community centers on wheels. The Army MPs, greeted with greater joy by the railroad than even higher earnings, have accomplished wonders. They see that both non-coms and officers dress properly for the diner and lounge. They prevent ardent young men from annoying fair ladies, halt excessive drinking and check on all passes, including those of sailors, Marines, Coast Guarders, Waves, Waacs and Spars.

'We don't call it AWOL when the ladies haven't got passes,' said a tall, blond MP, one of two on the train taking care of the 800 or so servicemen. 'That's known as "homesickness."'

He was a former bank clerk in New York, standing month after month in one tiled spot. Now he stands, but while the country speeds past him—Miami, Cleveland, Nashville, Boston—he's covered the East and South while walking the trains.

'We don't look for trouble,' he explained. 'That's the best way to avoid it.'

Yet they are judo trained, just in case. Their technique emphasizes politeness, followed by firmness. If a serviceman pulls out a flask for a 'quick snort,' the MP can make him pour the precious contents down the sink.

'But when we know a man has been overseas and is just back from fighting, sometimes we look the other way,' he confessed.

Civilians offer trouble, too. They often insist that a soldier take a drink when he has already had one too many. The MPs then appeal to the conductor for aid, as they are not allowed to argue with civilians.

As the train pulled into Grand Central Station, servicemen who'd had sufficient sleep energetically bustled into their belongings. Duffel bags flew through the smoky air, colliding with the valises of civilians. (The railroad would have all luggage checked for baggage-car shipment, but for mid-aisle sitting there's nothing like a suitcase for ballast.)

They flooded the platform and streamed up the ramp, Army and Navy topcoats banked by a few tweeds and furs. Station lights pierced sleepy eyes. The aerial photographer opened his eyes wide in wonder as we stepped into the vastness of the station.

'Nine days' furlough,' he breathed. 'Wow!'

That's what travel is for today.

—Lucy Greenbaum (1943)

AND ON TO WASHINGTON...

Two years after Lucy Greenbaum made her memorable journey from Boston to New York, the war was nearing its end, and times had changed. The nation and its people had become seasoned by the experience of global war.

When that crusty social critic WA Anderson had traveled to the nation's capital in 1942, the crowds were brash, excited, freshly uniformed, noisy, impatient and full of loud laughter. In May 1945, he recorded an older crowd, rich in experience,

Right: **Soldiers and civilians jam the Southern Pacific Station at the Oakland Pier— a scene that was repeated everywhere.**

purposeful, relaxed, traveling light, wearing uniforms 'as casually and comfortably as farmer's denim.' War was no longer a hysterical adventure. It was already history, with the first phase concluded, and the nation now turning with terrible but alert assurance to the war against Japan.

In 1945, Anderson had seen a soldier pressed in a corner of the soda counter of Union Station in Washington. Except for a service ribbon, there was nothing unusual about him in that crowd of fresh, unweathered people. But as he turned to move away, be hitched himself up on crutches. He had lost a leg. Then a strange thing happened. The crowd visibly opened before him. Laughter along his way broke off. People literally shied away, shocked at 'this unexpected apparition of the reality of things to come.'

A year later, within a hundred yards of this first war casualty, he'd seen two other casualties, hustling their own bags to the gates. One on crutches was being helped by a vigorous companion, a man of great physical energy and cheerful countenance. They were paratroopers, and the brisk, cheerful one was shifting their bags with two steel hooks 'where there had been strong hands a few months before. In the surge of weathered and battlewise soldiers, sailors and Marines, these two got no more than swift, understanding glances. They were confidently on their own.'

By 1945, the sensations of civilized living had 'shrunk to the proportions of little incidental ripples,' and the surging crowd saw with equal casualness a group of high-ranking bemedaled German officers pass through the station under experienced military escort, and 'a wild-eyed smuggler of heroin struggling like a trapped rabbit in the hands of the detectives.'

The experience of traveling by rail in wartime was not without both poignant and humorous moments. During one of Anderson's 1942 trips he noticed 'an unsalted Marine stimulated by corps traditions, trying to make time with a couple of brittle young women on their way to Chestnut Hill. His white cap was jaunty and his approach was brisk and assured, but it got him nowhere. They simply ignored him with a casual superiority he could not understand. Standing by their seat, he spoke with all conquering gaiety. Not only did they not hear him, they didn't even see him.'

In desperation, the Marine said, 'Maybe I'll be flying over Tokyo in a couple of weeks, and they won't even look at me!'

He was right, they wouldn't look at him. They got off at the 30th Street Station in Philadelphia and the Marine slumped morosely in his seat. At the time Anderson found him annoying, but now in Philadelphia, more than a year and a half later, he decided that the girls might have smiled. *Socially* they may have had local significance, but in the 'family of America' filling that car they were 'somehow foreign.'

More in harmony, Anderson felt, was the 'well groomed lady of uncertain years who said, with a gurgle of laughter, as she pushed out of the train at Washington, "Congratulate me! That sailor's winking!"'

The war years may have been the era in which the 'pin-up' came into its own as the art form most popular with servicemen, but it was also the era in which young ladies first learned the saying, 'The way to a man's heart is through his stomach.' WA Anderson recalled a big fellow with a European-African ribbon and a Purple Heart who sat beside him for two hours unsmilingly engrossed in a pile of comics. Suddenly he exploded with a roar of laughter. Pointing with stubby fingers, he thrust a series of

Left: **A smooth-talking soldier tries to engage a young lady in conversation as soldiers and civilians alike wait in line to purchase their tickets.**

three illustrations before Anderson. The first showed a large, forlorn sailor seated against a palm tree on an islet lost in the sea. In the second, the sailor had turned his head with an expression of wild delight as a lovely mermaid snuggled close to him. The third showed him in the same position, but looking out to sea with an expression of complete gratification. Beside him was a skeleton picked clean.

On another occasion, three veterans of the Pacific area, southward bound for Fort Bragg, occupied open seats across the aisle from Anderson. One was 'practical and energetic, and spent much of his time searching for the train butcher, who sold sandwiches and coffee.' Another was 'a sleepy, blue-eyed Virginian who sprawled contentedly in his seat, warm and happy, occasionally opening one eye for an all comprehending survey.' The third was 'an irrepressible romanticist, built for the movies and called "Frenchy."'

A trim and self-composed young lady, brown-eyed and comely, was seated behind Frenchy. The Virginian saw her first. He looked at Frenchy, and he looked over Frenchy's shoulder. Frenchy turned with a jerk and saw the girl; almost instantly he was on his knees on the seat, leaning over the back, talking to her. The Virginian lifted his face and closed his eyes with a contented smile.

Below: **Sailors fill the waiting room at the Pennsylvania Railroad's massive 30th Street Station in Philadelphia at the height of World War II.**

Soon Frenchy was seated beside the girl. By the time the train reached Wilmington, at the head of the Delaware Bay, their heads were together and they were talking in low, intimate tones, broken once by a shout, 'Boy, she's bound for Bragg!'

The sandwich hunter reappeared and stared dubiously at them. 'Going good,' the Virginian reported, opening an eye.

When the train pulled out of Baltimore, the girl had to freshen up for the change at Washington. As soon as she was out of hearing, Frenchy danced in the aisle, waving his arms with excitement. 'You guys listen to this. She's going to Bragg, too — and she can cook.'

The continuous stream of servicemen was like a broken army in all but spirit — straggling, clustering together, moving in swirling groups of Army, Navy and Marine uniforms of all ranks and grades, mingling with and almost overwhelming the hurrying civilians with their briefcases and bags, their babies, women and bundles.

To the girl in uniform, however, they all say 'Sister.' WA Anderson shared a seat with a WAC, a full technical sergeant — a woman with an air of kindly competence. She came from Scranton and she had a calm, even voice that must have inspired loyalty and respect among all who worked with her. They began speaking as the train swept over the narrow, unnoticed creek called Brandywine, and he pointed to the steely gleam that was the head of Chesapeake Bay — where the British fleet discharged

its army for a flanking march on Philadelphia, and on the western side to the hills behind which Washington had fought the Battle of the Brandywine.

She said she wished she could have had her son with her, because all this seemed so much like a story until you saw just where and how it happened.

'Where is your son?,' Anderson asked, since mothers are not usually acceptable for service.

She said he was in the Pacific. 'He's a regular,' she explained. She had worked to support him from his early childhood, and when he was seventeen, he asked permission to enlist.

'It was what he wanted,' she said, 'so I let him go. Usually he writes every week. Once a month before I joined up, he always sent me a little carton with flowers from Hawaii. I guess he's embarrassed now about mailing flowers to a sergeant.'

Generally, there was little by which to identify or localize individuals or groups. The uniforms and the wrinkled casualness of traveling outfits left few clues to location or occupation, to income or social and educational backgrounds. Yet the variety of individual characteristics is endless, and nostalgia for the home section was quickly evident after a few minutes of conversation.

Anderson had spent hours talking about the bevel of a plowshare with a New York farmer; of maple bush in Vermont; oyster pirating on the Chesapeake; the pile of arsenic under the big stack at Butte, Montana; the Western Quarter Horse and the Pennsylvania timber topper; Mississippi River boats; the smelt run in Michigan streams; lumbering on the Olympic Peninsula; and fishing on the Gulf.

'When I was a kid outside Galveston, we were always glad when the old man lost his job, because then we'd go fishing, and, boy, we began to live!'

There was a mild little fellow with big brown eyes and an oversized uniform whose seat Anderson had taken by mistake when the soldiers from Fort Dix moved out of the train at Trenton. An indignant family of fourteen beat upon the window and ordered Anderson away, and then he saw the soldier was saying farewell to his people, so he moved aside when the soldier returned. It was a night train, and they were both too sleepy to talk until Baltimore, where they arrived around midnight.

A couple of 'plump, overdressed women came aboard with loud laughter and shouts of drunken joy at the sight of relaxed soldiers.' They had no need of empty seats. They sat on the soldiers' laps with 'limp abandon and sentimental whoops.' The little soldier next to Anderson refused to warm to their advances, so they flung themselves upon a major and a colonel, who found small help from the shouted advice of the delighted ranks.

Anderson's GI explained to him, somewhat abashed, that he didn't want anything to do with *that* kind of woman.

'I got a nice family,' he said, 'and I love them.'

Wartime

The train was a local. At this particular dingy brick station it waited a long time. Through the smudged windows of the day-coach you could see a string of coal cars, the black tipple of a mine standing up in the fold of a hill beyond the bleak storefronts of the main street of the little town and behind the plum colored hills streaked with blue coal smoke.

On the worn brick pavement of the platform under the window, a group of people was gathered round a red-faced young soldier. He'd been home on leave and they had come to say goodbye. There was a gray-faced, stocky man in a dusty black hat with coal dust in his brows and lashes, who was evidently the father. There was the mother, a dumpy, pansy-faced woman with little wrinkles radiating from the corners of her eyes and mouth, looking quite crushed under a Sunday best coal scuttle hat of black velours. There was a lanky, careworn man in his shirt sleeves with two front teeth missing, who might be the older brother. There were some embarrassed small boys and an over dressed yellow-haired baby girl led by a noisy, busty woman in a picture hat, who was probably the sister-in-law.

Standing a little apart there was a skinny, large-eyed, thin-cheeked girl with skimpy blond hair who didn't seem to know what to do with a large new white handbag with spangly embroidery on it. The children looked forlorn, except for the small boy who was carrying the helmet, but the older people were all aggressively cheerful. The soldier was a well built young man who had the air of being the smartest and the best nourished and the best educated member of the family. He waved his arms and jumped about and kept up a continuous rattle of talk. Every sentence seemed to end with, 'And didn't we have a time?'

He told stories. He teased the kids. He grabbed his sister-in-law and started to show her how to do a new dance step. He ribbed his old man. He slapped his mother on the back. All the while he and the girl with the white handbag never dared look at one another.

When the brakeman shouted '*All aboard*,' and the engine bell started to clang, the GI grabbed his pack off the ground, took the tin hat off his little brother's head, and boarded the train with one leap. As he came down the aisle of the crowded coach the old man with drooping white mustaches and a kind of a Civil War veteran look in the seat in front of mine made room for him by letting him slip past into the place by the open window.

When he leaned out as the train began to move his broad khaki shoulders filled the window. He kept on laughing and shouting and even started telling a rambling story about an Irish sergeant who lost his boots.

He never got it finished. The train was rattling fast past the shacks and shanties on the edge of town before he pulled his head back into the car. He straightened his cap and sat there staring ahead of him, his face set and stiff and colorless.

The old man had been watching him. 'Son,' he said in a low conversational voice as if they'd been talking together for a long time. 'It reminds me of a story I used to hear when I was younger, about a famous clown... I don't rightly remember his name... a famous clown in the circus, who went through the whole show one night with a telegram in his pocket, and nobody in that immense audience noticed a thing. Indeed, some folks thought he was funnier than usual that night, and all the time he had a telegram in his pocket telling him that his little girl, his only child, was dead.'

—from *State of the Nation*
By John Dos Passos, 1944

Anderson mentioned that he'd seen some of his family at the window and the soldier had good reason to be proud. He warmed up then and said they were still all together, except for his brother, who'd been killed fighting Franco in Spain. At home, near Trenton, he said the family always got together on Saturdays, where they had a long wooden table under a grape arbor, and there they ate big bowls of Spanish food and drank wine and played the guitar and sang through the afternoon.

'By choice, I travel by coach,' Anderson wrote. 'The pontifical atmosphere of a Pullman, with its consciously important passengers either stiffly on guard or watching for influential contacts, puts me to sleep, but the lustiness and variety of the crowded coaches are an unfailing stimulant. Here the warm blood of America beats strongly.'

A sailor forcing his way through the pressing crowd in the aisle spotted the empty seat beside Anderson and threw a woman's suitcase down. 'Hold it, please!' he panted, and was off.

There appeared a 'plump and very pretty blonde with a sleeping baby straddled on her hip.'

The sailor shouted, 'Okay, mister, that's her!'

The bag was racked while Anderson held the baby, and the sailor found a place with shipmates down the aisle. Anderson commented to the girl that her husband knew how to look out for her. In a soft Carolina drawl, she said, 'Oh, those boys just adopted Jacky on the way up. I'm goin' to meet mah man in San Francisco comin' back from the South Seas.'

The train was hardly out of the yard, before she was again relieved of Jacky. He was, in Anderson's words, 'a lazy baby, whose curly head rolled as they picked him up and brought him to their seats.'

The girl told Anderson that she had come from her father's tidewater farm, where he fished and raised peanuts and sweet potatoes. 'You only had to look at her to know they lead a good and cheerful life down there,' he recalled. At Havre de Grace, where the Susquehanna River spreads out into the blue haze of the upper Chesapeake, she guessed it was time for Jacky's lunch. Without interrupting an account of how to make shrimp Norfolk, she opened her blouse for the nuzzling infant. This was a sailor's wife going to meet her husband, and 'safe in the care of

Below: **Southern Pacific's famous *Daylight* races through the California countryside on her run from San Francisco to Los Angeles.**

sailors from sea to sea, because they love her and all she represents.'

After the first hysterical phase of war excitement had waned late in 1942, there came a cold stiffness among the passengers. Anderson had noted that everyone became fearful of entering into conversation that might betray vital information. At night, window shades were drawn tight as each train left the Pennsylvania Station in New York and rushed south across the flat New Jersey plain. The interiors were gloomy with smoke and there was little conversation among the slumped figures pressed so closely together. This was in the days of the first convoys, when dark trains moved mysteriously in the night, and the *Limiteds* slowed to a stop or crawled hesitatingly at junctions where troops were moving toward embarkation points, and endless freight trains rumbled to the jumping off point for the Murmansk run and the African invasion.

By the coming of spring in 1944, however, self-conscious citizens and servicemen had acquired sophistication and skepticism. Conversations gradually became easy and general. The trainload was 'no longer a group of sensitive and suspicious individuals, but rather a family crowd, not greatly concerned with national policies, but tremendously interested in personal affairs.' Everywhere—in train stations and other public buildings—there were posters with grisly portrayals of ships destroyed by German U-Boats in the North Atlantic, which carried the grim admonishment, 'Loose Lips Sink Ships.'

One humorous incident that WA Anderson was to later recall involved a 'very solemn new ensign who came in with the rush of passengers at Philadelphia in the wake of a determined little bride with an orchid on her shoulder.' A roar of laughter followed them to the end of the car, where the young officer finally discovered a sign pinned on his back: 'Loose talk did this!'

All the words, all the books, all the pictures the mind and hands of man have recorded cannot encompass the pageant of the millions pouring and crowding into those cars that were shuttled back and forth at a mile a minute between the great cities of the Atlantic Seaboard. As WA Anderson recorded it in 1945, here was something the world had never known before—'a fusion of all nations, of all peoples, not into one typical race, but into one homogeneous congregation united by one political creed—government of the people, by the people for the people. Here were the people, traveling together.'

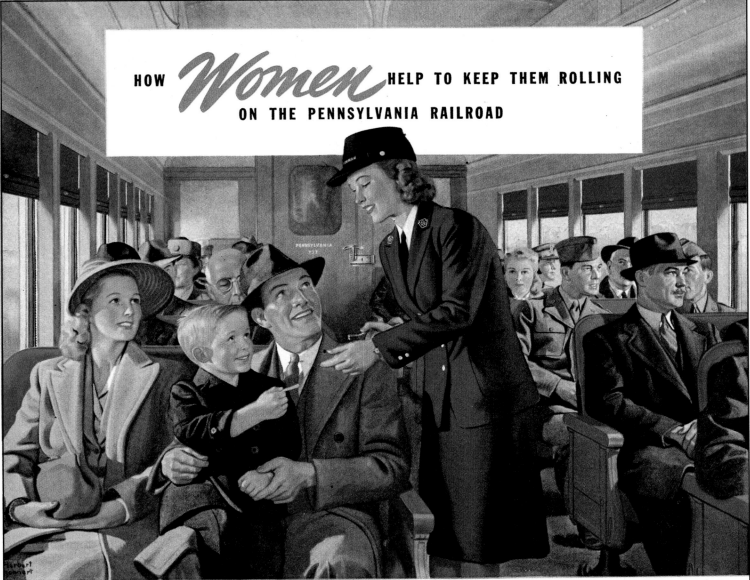

HOW *Women* HELP TO KEEP THEM ROLLING
ON THE PENNSYLVANIA RAILROAD

A WAR ROLE FOR WOMEN . . . as a trainman on the Pennsylvania Railroad. Women serve on short runs, as a rule.

RAILROADING has always been regarded as a man's calling.

But when war reached deeply into railroad ranks — taking from the Pennsylvania Railroad alone more than 41,000 skilled and experienced workers for the Armed Forces — women were employed to help keep trains rolling.

Today, on the Pennsylvania Railroad, approximately 22,000 women are serving in a wide variety of occupations—four of which you see illustrated here.

Positions such as trainmen, ticket sellers, train passenger representatives, ushers, information and reservation personnel call for intelligence, courtesy and a high degree of efficiency. Young women fresh from college and high school—after intensive training—have proved they can fill these roles most capably.

So, we're glad to have their help in the greatest job railroads have ever been called upon to do; *moving men and materials to Victory!*

AS A BRAKEMAN in freight yard operations, a woman fills a job that requires strength and coolness—in all weather.

AS AN USHER, a woman posts trains, announces departures and arrivals—answers the questions asked by travelers.

INFORMATION COUNTERS are besieged these days—so a woman's knowledge of travel must be extensive.

THE BEGINNING OF THE END

Just after World War II, the railroads were far from their plight of the Depression years, but there were already many disturbing omens. Though traffic in 1946 broke all peacetime records and was till straining war-battered facilities, it was considerably below the wartime peak and slipping fast. Competition from buses and airlines was getting stiffer and looked as if it would grow greater than ever. In 1941 the railroads operated nearly five times as many route miles as the airlines and two-thirds as many as the bus lines. However, in 1946 so many applications for new routes were on file by those competitors that the situation was reversed! New automobiles—which, in the final analysis, would be the railroads' biggest competitor for passenger transportation but which hadn't been built between 1942 and 1946 because of the war—were soon to roll off the assembly lines in huge quantities.

The infrastructure of the rail system was simply exhausted—worn out by the frantic and unprecedented pace and volume inflicted upon it by the war years. The Douglas DC-4 and DC-6 airliners of 1946 could carry more than twice as many passengers as the prewar DC-3s, and with four engines instead of just two, the new airliners could fly twice as far. Meanwhile, even larger airliners were coming into service. Lockheed's Constellations and Boeing's Stratocruisers could each carry as many people as five DC-3s, and hence, they made air travel not only faster and more reliable than it had been in 1939, but also much cheaper for travelers, while at the same time being more *profitable* for the airlines.

Concurrently, operating costs for the railroads were skyrocketing so fast that in 1946 most railroads began to lose—at an alarming rate—the fat they had accumulated during the booming war years. Bigger payrolls had added an estimated $680 million in expenses in 1946, and increases in fuel and material costs added up to $193 million more. Prices for new equipment the railroads needed so badly were escalating so fast that some equipment manufacturers refused to sign contracts stating exact prices. In 1945 the Class I railroads—those with annual operating revenues of $1 million or more each, and which operated 95 percent of the total railway mileage in the United States—had a net income of $447 million. For 1946, this dropped to $203 million, of which $174 million came not from actual operating income during that year, but from tax carry-back credits. For 1947, they foresaw a deficit of $312 million before carry-back credits, or $225 million after deducting those credits. For the first time in its 100-year history, the great Pennsylvania Railroad faced a deficit for the full year of 1946.

The Pullman Company—after vociferously denying that there was any black market in railroad reservations, or that it was necessary to bribe conductors and other railroad employees to get reservations—put into effect a 24-hour deadline for canceling reservations without penalty—a move which made it financially risky for black market operators and dishonest employees to juggle reservations.

As historian David Wittels pointed out, the railroads didn't ask for increases in passenger rates. *They didn't dare!* They might have been able to cite convincing figures in support of such a plea, however, because a major part of their competitive position then rested on being cheaper than the airlines and remaining within 'hailing distance' of bus fares. They had come to the conclusion that the only way they could make money on their passenger business was to get plenty of passengers and keep them.

Though they knew they couldn't compete with the airlines on the basis of speed, the railroads stepped up schedules. Both the Pennsylvania and the Santa Fe, the two largest railroads in the United States, made surveys and improvements in their lines that pointed toward potential 100 mph speeds. Before World War II, Santa Fe's fastest Chicago-Los Angeles train—the *Chief*—took 68 hours and 15 minutes. In 1946, Santa Fe's *Super Chief* and

Below: **What's wrong with this picture? Yes, it's a DC-4 in Santa Fe Colors! The Santa Fe Skyway, ironically offered only *freight* service. *Facing page:* The hope and promise of the postwar world as symbolized by a returning sailor, his beaming bride and their new baby aboard Southern Pacific's *Daylight* in December 1945.**

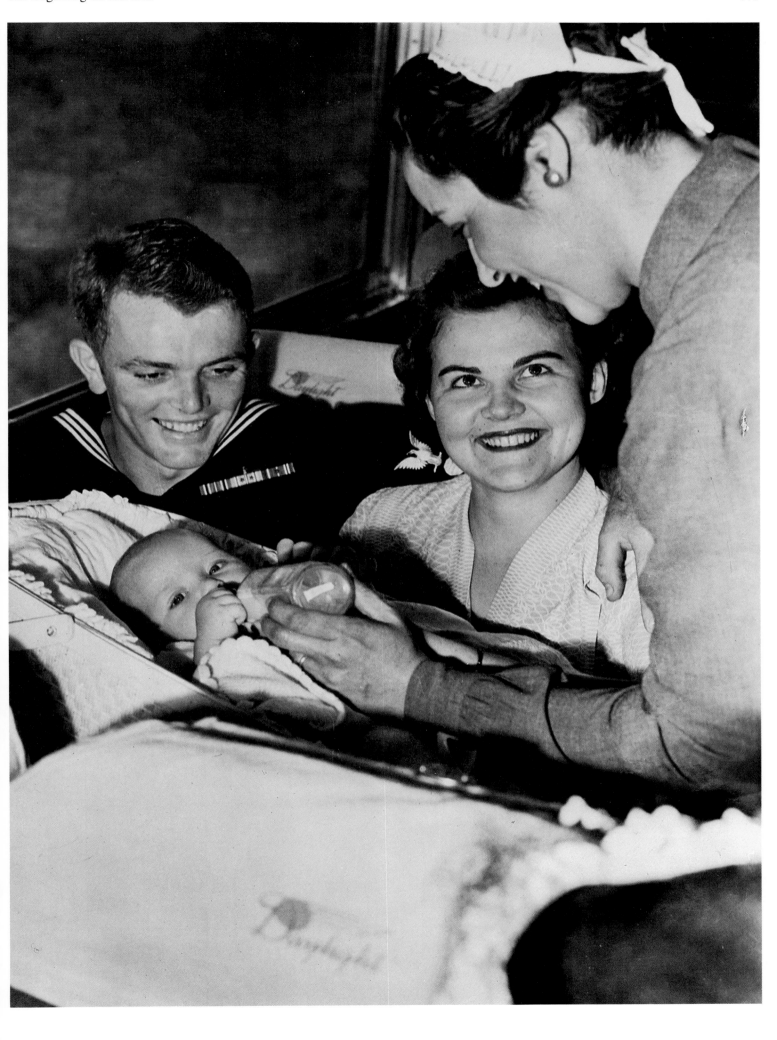

El Capitan did it in 39 hours and 45 minutes. The Pennsylvania's *Congressional*, which used to take four hours and 40 minutes for the 226-mile New York-Washington run, did it in the spectacular time of three and a half hours. When the Pere Marquette put the first postwar trains on the Detroit-Lansing-Grand Rapids run, it cut 40 minutes, or 20 percent, from the previous fastest time of three hours and 20 minutes.

During the war, the railroads had performed prodigious feats of transportation, which even the experts would have said were impossible. Before the war, for instance, the Pennsylvania used to gird itself for days ahead when it faced what seemed like the gargantuan job of moving 100,000 people between New York and Washington on an inaugural day or the day of a big football game. It considered it necessary to shunt its freight trains out of the way on such days. During the war, however, the Pennsylvania found itself hauling more than 100,000 passengers on that run every day (with a peak of 159,000 one day) without having to shunt *any* of its *record-breaking* freight traffic out of the way. Despite these incredible achievements, the challenges the railroads faced in 1946 would ultimately prove insurmountable.

In addition to the obvious method of adding more ticket windows, experiments were first made with electrical ticket vending machines 'which can make change and do practically everything except point the way to the restrooms,' Wittels noted. There were also plans for more attractive waiting rooms, such as the sumptuous, clublike women's lounge in the Chicago Union Station. Baggage handling procedures of a type familiar today to airline passengers was also introduced in 1946. Passengers were relieved of their luggage the moment they entered a station. It was then labeled according to terminal points, stowed out of the way aboard the trains and handed politely to the patrons as they left their stations. For the first time in American history, it was possible to travel from coast to coast without being thrown off one train, baggage and all, and clambering aboard a second train at Chicago.

By the end of the 1940s, however, domestic airlines would soon capture the bulk of first-class, inter-city passenger traffic as a result of steadily increasing railroad fares. The railroads, which handled about 90 percent of the first-class common carrier passenger business via Pullman and parlor car as late as 1945, retained less than 60 percent of the traffic in 1949, and by the next year, the airlines had captured close to half of the first-class travel market.

Prospects for a continual decline in rail passenger business were heightened by the Interstate Commerce Commission's 1949 decision granting 61 eastern railroads a 12.5 percent fare boost. This increase—the third since the war—brought basic rail coach fares east of the Mississippi and north of the Ohio and Potomac rivers to 3.375 cents a mile and parlor and sleeping car rates to more than 4.5 cents a mile, which made them almost twice as high as bus fares and slightly above the air coach level between many cities.

Airline penetration of the total first-class market increased from 11 percent in 1945 to 34.5 percent in 1948, and to over

Easy Does It...when the family goes New York Central

Easy on Dad! No traffic to tire him. No white line to watch. When New York Central does the driving, he's free to read, nap, or enjoy the wonderful *Water Level Route* scenery that parades past his big picture window.

Easy on Mother, because her mind's at ease about the youngsters. No back-seat fidgets. No frequent roadside stops. Everything the children need is right at hand. And they couldn't be safer at home!

Easy on the Kids! They don't have to stay put in their seats. There's plenty of room to move about. And there's the extra thrill of those famous New York Central meals in the diner, with their own, thrifty Children's Menu to choose from.

Easy on the Budget! Round-trip coach fares are low. And special Family Tickets cut them as much as 50% or even more. Ask your New York Central ticket agent all about them.

New York Central
The Scenic Water Level Route

EWEST EVENT ON AMERICA'S NEW RAILROAD

New Luxury Service for Coach-Fare Travel Chicago-Los Angeles

Goes into operation in midsummer

The instant you see it, you'll know this train is different. It's high—designed to provide smoother rides, more room, and b panoramic views of Southwestern scenery. "Upstairs"—well the clickety-clack of the rails—are foam-rubber reclining sea full-length legrests, big picture windows, dining room, and l lounge. "Downstairs" are luggage racks and washrooms. Courier Nurse service. Indian Guide, westbound across Ne Fred Harvey meals. You'll be riding high, wide and hands new all-coach *El Capitan!* Extra fare $5.00, Chicago—Los Watch your local newspapers for the date it goes into servie

R. T. Anderson, General Passenger Traffic Manager, Chicago

Above: The famous Louisville & Nashville Railroad passenger train *The Humming-bird,* crossing Biloxi Bay in 1946. Although railroad traffic broke peacetime records in 1946, the year signaled the beginning of the end for the industry.

40 percent in 1949. Total revenue passenger miles flown by the airlines soared from $1.4 billion in 1941 to $3.3 billion in 1945, and to $6.5 billion in 1949. By contrast, first-class, inter-city passenger mileage rose from 9.2 billion in 1941 to 26.9 billion in 1945, and fell back to 9.2 billion in 1949. Rail coach traffic increased from 16.1 billion revenue miles in 1941 to to 59.4 billion in 1945, but then slid to 23 billion in 1949.

With a minimum of publicity, some crack train schedules were canceled or consolidated with other trips as a result of falling patronage. Plans for buying new luxury passenger equipment were shelved.

However, it was the private automobile which proved to be the greatest challenge to airlines, buses and railroads alike in the passenger field. In 1941 the common carriers handled only about 13.2 percent of all inter-city travel, with automobiles carrying the rest. During 1944, when wartime gas rationing was in effect, the common carriers took care of 44 percent of the total passenger business, but this percentage dropped to 26.2 percent in 1946, and steadily declined to only 15 percent by 1949.

Between 1941 and 1949, airline fares (based on receipts per passenger mile) rose from 5.01 cents to 5.8 cents—an increase of 15.7 percent. In 1949, one-way rail Pullman fares (for a lower berth) from New York to Chicago were $48.64, compared to $44.10 for regular airline flights. Rail coach tickets between the same two points were $30.71, compared to $29.60 by airplane.

Faced by a rapid dwindling from the wartime traffic peak and by stiffer postwar competition from airplanes, buses and private automobiles, the railroads began paying sharp attention to rider surveys. As one observer noted in 1949, 'The public, fed up with being jammed into crummy old atrocities and ending long train rides feeling as if beaten with sticks, is demanding more comfort and at a low cost.'

The attitude of courtesy entered the lexicon of the passenger service of the railroad companies in the postwar years that caught many a rider off guard. Historian David Wittels described it in a particularly witty anecdote. Citing an instance in which he'd had to telephone for some timetable information, he realized that he was 'accustomed to hearing the ring signal *br-r-r-ring* vainly for from three to fifteen minutes, while the clerks polished their nails or discussed the fourth race at Jamaica.' However, he 'almost dropped the phone when a polite voice answered immediately.' When the voice, instead of 'growling or cutting me off with my question only half answered, gave the information as if it was a pleasure and wound up by saying, "Thank you for calling, sir," Wittels concluded that 'Maybe the railroads were here to stay after all.'

This 'new thoughtfulness' for the comfort of even low-paying coach passengers was also exemplified in the pains taken in designing the cars for the coaches of the future. Though Wittels' optimistic supposition was ultimately incorrect, at that time the railroads *were* trying.

Below: **Vacationers enjoyed the scenic beauty of the Southwest during a 1946 trip to Palm Springs via the Southern Pacific.**

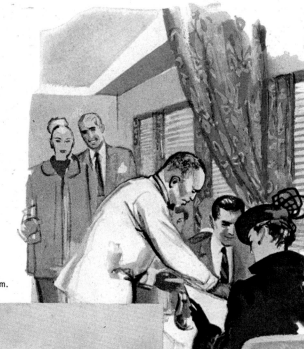

Great Northern's legendary *Empire Builder (below)* on her run from Seattle to Everett, Washington. Imagine what it would be like to have Puget Sound outside your window!

THE TRAIN OF THE FUTURE

One way of dealing with current problems is to predict a rosy future, and so it was with the rail passenger industry in the late 1940s. There was an abundance of innovations and countless predictions. Among the latter was the image conjured up by Ralph Haman, an engineer with the Pullman-Standard Car Manufacturing Company.

As David Wittels described it, Ralph Haman was fond of saying that he was born in a railroad station, and that was literally true. His father was the station agent at McConnell, Illinois, a whistle stop on the Illinois Central, so the agent and his family lived on the second floor of the railroad station. When Haman was born in 1901, a freight train was chugging past not twenty feet from his mother's bedroom window. When he was a small boy, his father would hand him up to the engineer of a passing train, who would ride him in the cab some 50 miles up the line and then turn him over to the engineer of a train heading back.

It was natural, therefore, that Haman should grow up to be a railroad man; and it was natural, too, that when he found himself with nothing much else to do one day in February 1940, he should begin 'doodling pictures of railroad trains.' Pretty soon the touch of 'attic madness,' which is the hallmark of practically all designers—Haman had by now become a famous train designer—took hold of him, and he conjured up a vision in a 1946 book called *The Trainwave* and subtitled *The Train of 1990*.

It was, as Wittels puts it, 'a utopian train, with Buck Rogers overtones.' So completely streamlined that from above it resembled a segmented snake, it would zip through the countryside at 200 mph. Within its soundproofed, circular interior there would be a movie and television theater, private club rooms for games and conferences, a beauty parlor, a barbershop, private baths, a playroom to keep tot-sized travelers out of the other customers'

hair, radio telephones and a night club in which to drink and dance the miles away. The air conditioning would be so perfect that not a speck of dust could get in, and the temperature would always be between 68 and 70 degrees. Luggage would disappear into hidden receptacles, a trained nurse would change diapers and dispense hangover remedies, obsequious valets would press travel-creased clothes, and the washrooms would be spacious, spotless and plentiful. No one would have to bribe a conductor to get a seat or a bed.

Practically everything on this marvelous train would be 'push button controlled and automatic. Electric-eye gadgets would open and close all doors, adjust the beds and seats, and operate the toilet facilities. The roofs of the sleeping cars would be sheathed in a special glass which filtered out the harmful rays and intensified the beneficial ones.'

However, as historian Wittels also points out, 'This magnificent conception almost got Haman blacklisted in the trade when it came to the attention of a couple of the more literal-minded railroad executives of the old school. They were afraid that the design might get into the hands of the public and lead the public to expect utterly impossible things.'

The 'Trainwave' was indeed a preposterous train, as Haman knew very well. Even if the three-way ball bearing suspension stunt could work, which was problematical, the job would mean rebuilding the $21 billion railroad plant almost from scratch: thousands of new locomotives, nearly 50,000 new passenger cars, tens of thousands of new bridges and tunnels, and

Right: Two or three of the 'world's lightest highballs' and one was ready for a tomorrow that included a rocket-propelled monorail 'highballing' down the Susquehanna. Ralph Haman *(see text)* dreamed the dream, but his 'tomorrow' has waited a half century unfulfilled. *Below:* The great Pennsy electrics of Haman's era are, ironically, more streamlined than the 'streamliners' of the 1980s.

Men Who Think of Tomorrow Appreciate The World's Lightest Highball !

Men Who Think of Tomorrow

What will the train of the future be like? Will a single rail and airplane designing give it a speed of 200 . . . 300 miles per hour? Ask the men who are thinking today about the "rocket" train of *Tomorrow!*

*   *   *

Seagram's foresight—*Seagram* thought of Tomorrow, the year "Monopoly" was played in a million homes; the year the Townsend Plan was announced; the year King George V celebrated his Silver Jubilee. That's when the rare whiskies for Seagram's V.O. CANADIAN were expertly blended and laid away to mellow. Today, as always, we are storing fine whiskies for Tomorrow—so you may always enjoy this glorious Seagram's V.O.—famed as the whisky that *tastes better* —preferred for the world's lightest highball!

Seagram's V.O. CANADIAN
CANADIAN WHISKY • A BLEND OF RARE SELECTED WHISKIES

Seven Years Old — 86.8 Proof. Seagram-Distillers Corporation, New York

The quest for innovation in the late 1940s produced a new kind of locomotive. It still used coal and water to produce steam, but the steam did not turn the wheels directly. Instead the steam generated electricity for electric motors mounted on the axles. To contain all this equipment, The Baldwin Locomotive Works and Westinghouse Electric Corporation constructed the world's longest—154 feet—passenger locomotive for the Chesapeake & Ohio Railroad (below). C & O was so pleased with this futuristic 1947 locomotive that it ordered two more.

nearly 400,000 miles of elevated, special track.

Haman had only been daydreaming, but though his Trainwave was 'strictly a gag,' in creating this chimera he wove his fantasy around improvements which he knew the railroads themselves were planning for the 1950s and which they had already designed and were scheduled to roll out of the shops 'as soon as materials become available.'

The 1946 view of 'tomorrow trains' predicted that they would be as different from the 'dingy, dilapidated rolling stock into which passengers were jammed during the war period as some of the movie palaces of the late 1940s were from nickelodeons of the 1920s. There will be trains with movies, nursery playrooms, night clubs and parlor cars like gracious living rooms instead of the stuffy, grim accommodations now in use.' Pullman already had such cars in mock-up form and was taking orders for them in 1946. There would be 'dining cars with elbowroom, windows with heated glass, free libraries, soft music, loud speaker announcements of points of interest and no luggage underfoot. Coaches would have individual reclining chairs, push button operated, which, with with built-in, ample footrests, would create a chaise lounge effect for practically full-length reclining. There would be closets for coats, wraps and parcels, and individual reading lights and muted radio speakers built into the seats at ear level. Coach trains would include dressing rooms, and recreation cars, or rumpus rooms for card games, parties and songfests en route. All these trains would, of course, be streamlined and air-conditioned, and have glareless, shadowless lighting, murals, reasonable soundproofing and bigger and more washrooms.'

Pullman predicted that there would be stewardesses, maids, barbers, valets, telephones and shower baths. Some crack extra-fare trains—such as the Santa Fe's *Super Chief*—already had such baronial touches, but these services were confidently forecasted to become more common.

Meanwhile, however, the Edward G Budd Manufacturing Company was developing a car which embodied at least a first cousin, whimsical idea: a car which can be considered the last great innovation of the golden age of rail travel. This car, the Vista-Dome, was a deluxe coach with a glass compartment rising out of the roof. Within this dome, which somewhat resembled the 'blister,' or the nose, of a huge bombing plane, were 24 seats from which passengers could view the passing scenery from a lordly height. The Chicago, Burlington & Quincy described it as a 'penthouse view.' At night, only the floor lights were left on, creating an effect 'eerily like that of soaring through space.'

At least a dozen other railroads were also planning to use such cars, some of which would double as parlor-observation cars. Further, it was confidently projected that there would be no more 'old-fashioned sleeping cars with the drab curtains buttoning across berths designed for a race of contortionists, the stepladders to the uppers, and the dreary morning line ups *en d'shabille*, at the inadequate washrooms.'

Robert R Young, postwar America's 'daring young man of Wall Street,' moved into the railroad business with a blaze of new ideas, publicly blasting the old cars as 'rolling tenements.' However, Young was 'shooting at already dying game.' The railroads were not ordering any more of these 'torture chambers.' In fact, they were eager to replace existing rolling stock with new day/night coaches and with cars containing ingeniously modified roomettes that would cost the traveler 'little, if any, more than a berth.'

However, though hundreds of super deluxe coaches of the

Integrated Transportation Center by Men Who Plan beyond Tomorrow!

PLANNING TODAY FOR TOMORROW'S TRAVEL

Many enterprising communities are planning post-war to concentrate all forms of transportation in one great center at the edge of town...a combined airport, railroad station, bus terminal. Freight will be handled speedily between trains and platforms, where trucks and trailers can load or unload. Ample parking space for private automobiles.

YESTERDAY'S PLANNING FOR TODAY'S PLEASURE

The youngest whiskies in Seagram's V.O. Canadian, were laid away six years ago...the year Franco won the Spanish Civil War, the year "Gone With The Wind" had its movie premiere in Atlanta, and "Life With Father" started its record run. Today enjoy the mellow lightness of Seagram's V.O.

Six Years Old—86.8 Proof. Seagram-Distillers Corporation, New York

Seagram's V.O. CANADIAN

CANADIAN WHISKY—A BLEND....OF RARE SELECTED WHISKIES

Above: Seagram's pipedream of an Integrated Transportation Center on the site of today's San Francisco Airport was dashed by a half century of regional provincialism, petty politics and Byzantine county planning codes. No rail service yet reaches the airport, but the parking garage *sort of* looks like this.

'trains of tomorrow' were on the order books of Pullman-Standard, Budd and the American Car & Foundry Company in 1946, it was estimated that it would be 'at least a couple of years' before they become common sights. This lag was seen as mainly being due to the continuing shortage of materials in the wake of World War II and to a US government order giving first priority on available materials to high-capacity coaches. That order made sense, in view of the desperate need for 'any kind of serviceable coaches' to replace the cars worn out under the beating of wartime traffic, but it blocked out 'for the time being' the newest models in which the luxury touches would obviously cut down the number of seats.

In 1945 and 1946, the railroads were forced to order those types of cars which they could get fastest, mostly prewar models. They committed themselves to about $1.6 billion worth of new equipment in 1946, with the New York Central alone ordering nearly 800 passenger cars at a cost of nearly $60 million, and the Pennsylvania ordering about $50 million worth of cars and locomotives. The first coach trains truly indicative of 'what to expect when the trains of tomorrow come' were delivered to the Pere Marquette in August 1946.

The glamour cars, such as the movie and night club cars, the rumpus cars, the children's playrooms, would be 'even longer delayed.' None were built in1946, and most railroads proceeded cautiously to see how far they would have to incorporate luxury touches to keep other forms of transportation from luring their customers away.

Illustrated is the new, Budd-built Vista Dome car ordered by several railroads. The first of these revolutionary new cars are being delivered to the Burlington Lines for the new Twin Cities Zephyrs for service between Chicago and St. Paul-Minneapolis.

The New Budd Trains are Rolling

At an increasing pace, The Budd Company is delivering new stainless steel trains to the nation's foremost railroads.

They are causing major readjustments in the way people think about traveling.

For these trains demonstrate that travel is more than simply a means of getting from one place to another. They offer a new experience in happy living . . . an experience that puts the emphasis where it belongs—on safety and pleasure, with speed an incidental.

Many, many new conveniences and perfected appointments contribute to this feeling. But basic to the beauty, the luxury and the security of these new Budd-built stainless steel trains is the planned purpose to make rail travel the most enjoyable way to go places, no matter how little or how much you can afford to spend.

These new Budd trains are playing an important role in the American railroads' vast modernization program, and are taking top rank among their famous "blue ribbon" fleets. Trains most recently equipped by Budd are:

ADVANCE SILVER METEOR

CHAMPION	**SILVER COMET**
MAN O' WAR	**SILVER METEOR**

Mounting deliveries will soon add many more illustrious names to the list of Budd-built stainless steel streamliners. The Budd Company, Philadelphia.

One version of the 'train of tomorrow' was the electric locomotive. This Great Northern locomotive *(below)*—at one time the largest single-cab electric locomotive in the world—ran through the Cascade tunnel in western Washington.

THE ECONOMICS OF
'THE NEW THOUGHTFULNESS'

There was a high price to pay in meeting postwar competition, not only in terms of technology, but in service as well. To respond to the challenge from the airlines, the railroads did what they could to improve the quality of their service. By 1954, a major renovation of the dining car—the essential element of rail travel—had taken place.

On many American railroads, dining car service had remained pretty much unchanged since the era of the buffalo steak. What happened in the early 1950s represented a trend toward economy, efficiency and—some 'romantics' feared—the sacrifice of much of the color and atmosphere that once inspired the average American to regard a meal on the 'the diner' as one of his most exciting eating experiences.

'The truth about this business,' a dining executive said at the time, 'is this: The fewer people we can manage to feed on a railroad dining car, the lower our losses are.' Yet the railroads didn't try to *discourage* people from eating, as one might have imagined from this statement, but sought to apply efficiency methods to a feeding operation that had a tradition of extravagance.

Shrewd operational reforms embraced everything from the adoption of smaller dinner plates—to make the smaller steaks *look* larger—to dyeing waiters' coats green. (Green coats can be sorted more efficiently at the laundry and also require fewer washings than white ones.)

The Pennsylvania Railroad became so efficiency-minded that

Below: **Aboard the Southern Pacific's *Coast Daylight* in 1952. The decade of the 1950s saw a rethinking of the railroad industry's past policies and procedures. In answer to the growing competition from the airlines, the railroads turned to cost-saving measures, particularly on the dining cars.**

In an era of cutbacks, Santa Fe was one of the few railroads that continued its tradition of fine dining aboard its luxury trains. *Below:* This sleek hi-level Santa Fe passenger train streaked through the rich agricultural countryside of southern California in the 1950s.

Travel Comfort on the Santa Fe

Young or old, you'll like traveling on Santa Fe trains. They're downright comfortable!

You choose from a wide variety of accommodations ... get plenty of room to roam. Dressing rooms are spacious.

You board your train downtown ... leave on schedule in any weather ... enjoy wonderful Fred Harvey meals en route ... arrive relaxed, refreshed.

And on the *Texas Chief, El Capitan* and *The Grand Canyon*, an alert and capable Courier-Nurse (registered graduate nurse) is aboard to help those who need her friendly service.

For the utmost in travel comfort, go Santa Fe *all the way*.

Santa Fe

Ride great trains through a great country

R. T. Anderson, General Passenger Traffic Manager, Santa Fe System Lines, Chicago 4

it began to make its own lard from fat scraps. No longer did New York Central crews eat from the passenger menu. The railroad fed them on less expensive chow, such as ribs, round meat or frankfurters. The calculating machine became almost as important as the refrigerator in railroad commissary departments.

By 1954, on some trains, like New York Central's *Empire State Express*, which ran from New York to Cleveland, the snowy napery of yore had been replaced by paper doilies and napkins and sandwiches were served on paper plates. Such economies allowed the diners to cut prices by one-third; and the New York Central reduced its loss on the run by using three instead of six waiters. The New York Central and several other railroads attempted to introduce a complete frozen dinner that could be whipped out of the ice chest and 'cooked' in a precursor of the mircrowave oven of the future, but the patrons wouldn't buy it even at a come-on price of 99 cents. Its time had not yet arrived.

A few trains installed sandwich and drink vending devices, either to replace or to supplement regular dining cars. But what proved to be the greatest shock to old-time riders turned up in 1953 on the Atchinson, Topeka & Santa Fe's *California Limited*: a cafeteria car. The menu included three entrees, like veal cutlet, baked ham or pot roast, at 75 cents each; three styles each of vegetables and potatoes, three salads and three desserts. A complete dinner cost about $1.50. Some 20 percent of the passengers complained about the cafeteria, but the railroad claimed that it was patronized by 40 to 45 percent of the coach passengers aboard. Also, whereas previously fewer than 30 percent of the coach passengers ever ventured into the regular diner, Pullman passengers continued to prefer the diner. As in the past, the Fred Harvey Company—the firm founded by Santa Fe's famed caterer—kept the dream alive. On fancier trains like the *Chief* or *Super Chief*, imported Irish linen and quadruple-plate silver continued to be used.

In the cafeteria car, only three passengers aboard the *California Limited* dropped their trays during the first six months of its operation. What was more interesting to the Santa Fe Railroad, however, was the fact that the cafeteria could be run with seven employees—a steward, chef-dish-up-man, two helpers, a 'yard man' to clean up and two bus men—instead of a regular diner crew of 10. It cost $2000 less a month to operate. Even so, the cafeteria continued to cost the railroad $1.25 for every dollar of revenue.

During 1952, 37 railroads belonging to the American Association of Railroad Dining Car Users served 37,827,633 passenger meals. The revenue was $59,602,288, but the meals cost the railroads over $75 million, for a net revenue loss of more than $15 million. Without economies, the deficit would have been nearer $24 million. About 80 million meals were served that year by all railroads, but only one showed a profit from diners: the Chicago North Shore and Milwaukee, a short-run electric line. It served more liquor than food and restricted its menus to the simplest items. Each car was manned by just one waiter in charge, so that nonproductive time was only an hour between runs.

In 1920, the Pennsylvania Railroad served four million meals, at a loss of $932,000. In 1946, it lost over $5 million on 7.3 million meals. In 1952, the deficit was $3.5 million on 4.5 million meals. This loss probably would have been $1.56 million greater without the railroad's economy measures. Most railroads never tried economizing until after World War II, when diner losses began mounting, while at the same time freight revenues began declining.

In 1952, although the number of riders decreased, the per-

centage of those using the diners increased. One out of every three passengers on the Louisville & Nashville line used the diners, whereas in 1930 dining cars attracted only one passenger in 15. The explanation for this growth is simple: lengths of rides increased—an average L & N ride in 1928 had been 195 miles, up from 69 miles in 1926—and passengers naturally got hungrier. Another factor was the virtual disappearance of the old box lunch. During the early 1950s, with the one exception of the crushing diner patronage during World War II, dining cars were more likely to be full than at any other time in railroad history.

Broken crockery was another factor that added to the expense of operating a diner. In an average month, the Pennsylvania Railroad had to replace 2480 broken cups, 758 tea plates, 1103 consommé cups, 588 grapefruit dishes, 889 pudding dishes, 50 platters, 474 rimmed fruit dishes, 3528 salad plates, 1527 dinner plates, 1877 saucers and 123 soup plates.

The biggest expense, however, was crew salaries. Waiters earned 31 cents an hour in 1941, but by 1953 this had climbed to $1.36 an hour. A diner requires twice as large a crew as a restaurant to serve a given number of people. In addition to salaries, on overnight runs the train had to furnish food and lodging for the crews. Each month the Pennsylvania served an average of 62,500 meals to diner employees, compared to 400,000 revenue meals.

To economize, after consulting records that show what percentage of the passengers aboard would eat in the diner on that particular day of the week, the railroad would decide how many men were needed in the dining crew. The heaviest dining car days, in order, were Friday, Thursday, Sunday, Wednesday, Monday, Tuesday and Saturday. Depending on the day of the week and the number of its passengers, the size of the *Congressional Limited*'s diner crew varied from 10 to 16 men—a payroll difference of about $100 a day.

In 1952 the Pennsylvania removed some seats from one end of a coach and installed sandwich and drink vending machines. Encouraged by the small profit these made, the railroad instituted an Automatic Café Bar Car in the coach end of two Washington-New York trains. Each of these cars was a 1909-style coach remodeled to contain a 17-foot stand-up bar at one end and some coach seats at the other. In the center was an automatic restaurant consisting of four tables, 16 seats and various automatic devices that vended sandwiches, candy bars, juices, ice cream, milk, coffee and cigarettes.

In the mid-1950s, most larger railroads that had economy programs spent around $1.30 for every dollar they took in on diner sales. A few others—including the Baltimore and Ohio, the Chicago, Milwaukee, St Paul & Pacific, and the Northern Pacific—apparently felt that food was a railroad's best advertisement, and didn't do much economizing. Food costs per dollar of sales for this group ranged from $1.47 for the Chicago & North Western, up to $1.87 on the Union Pacific.

Old-time dining car waiters observed these changes with growing apprehension. They appeared to portend fewer jobs and were seen as the beginning of the end of an era. Their attitude was well summarized by a dream a Pennsylvania Railroad waiter had about Maynard A Ingram who, as personnel chief, had responsibility for reducing diners' crew to fit the number of passengers on a given day.

'I dreamed about you last night, Mr Ingram,' the waiter told him. 'You was dead, and some of us waiters were the pall-bearers. Just as we were taking you up the church steps, you sat up in the coffin and said, "Boys, there is too many of you on this coffin. Lay a couple off. Six of you can carry me to Glory just as easy as eight."'

© 1947 P-S. C. M. Co.

Gateways to Safe and Pleasant Journeys

To the rail terminals of American cities come the famous trains whose names spell the romance of travel. To these stations come travelers, in ever increasing numbers, who appreciate the dependability and luxurious comfort of a fine train... of cars built by Pullman-Standard.

If you want to go when you plan to go... if you enjoy *eye-level* scenery, relaxation and fun en route, you'll *go by train*. If you look for the finest and safest in rail transportation, you'll find it on cars which bear the Pullman-Standard nameplate.

By placing passenger comfort and safety first; by setting the pace in engineering and design; by leadership in quality and volume of production, Pullman-Standard has helped American railroads lead the world in low-cost, safe, luxurious transportation.

Because of *quality*—proven in long years of fine carbuilding—the railroads have bought most of their modern, streamlined passenger cars from Pullman-Standard.

PULLMAN-STANDARD CAR MANUFACTURING COMPANY
CHICAGO, ILL. · OFFICES IN SIX CITIES FROM COAST TO COAST
MANUFACTURING PLANTS AT SIX STRATEGIC POINTS

World's largest builders of streamlined railroad cars... **PULLMAN-STANDARD**

THE UNEXCELLED GRANDEUR of the Canadian Rockies is in full view above, behind and all around you when you ride THE CANADIAN's luxurious Scenic D

Canadian Pacific presents Canada's spectacular panorama from

Imagine yourself in this setting—aboard this train.

Literally surrounded by natural splendor you speed across Canada in ultra-modern luxury. For 2,881 breathtaking miles you ride in royal comfort, command service unsurpassed in rail travel whether you go coach, tourist or first class.

You dine graciously in a Deluxe Dining Room Car or take your meals informally in the Skyline Coffee Shop. You sip refreshments in an intimate Mural Lounge or relax in a roomy and beautifully appointed Observation Lounge.

Aboard spacious coaches (on which all seats are reserved) you ride comfortably in reclining armchairs with full-length leg rests and adjustable head rests. And each car on THE CANADIAN has its own unique décor, its own restful charm delightfully enhanced by the unobtrusive tones of transcribed music.

In daily service between Montreal and V and Toronto and Vancouver, THE CANADI you the longest dome ride in the world, ca comfortably across Canada under smooth dies

Plan your trip now. THE CANADIAN's tren successful maiden year of operation has created of excited comment. Service aboard THE CA

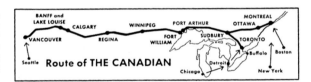

LIFE IN THE DINING CAR

On overnight trains, the dining car day began as the third cook started the kitchen fire at 4:30 am. The rest of the crew would awake 30 minutes later.

Dining car crews usually reported for duty four or five hours before the big overnight trains pulled out to prepare roasts, most of the bread and vegetables and all the desserts. The cooking that was done after the train journey began was usually confined to steaks, chops, short orders or perhaps some special dish, such as game, that passengers may have brought aboard.

In the age of efficiency that marked the end of the golden age in the 1950s, the number of waiters on a train ranged from one on a club car to 10 on some big twin units. The latter consisted of an 84-foot diner, adjoined by a similar length car containing the pantry, kitchen and a lounge on daylight trains, like the Pennsyl-

vania's *Congressional Limited*. On overnight trains like the *Twentieth Century Limited*, the crew quarters were alongside the kitchens and passenger lounges were located elsewhere. A twin unit cost about $400,000. It carried $6500 worth of portable equipment—2500 pieces of linen and 2500 other pieces of silver, china and glass. On an overnight trip it would carry about $650 worth of food and $150 worth of liquor.

The chef also handled roasts, soups, sauces and the inventory of supplies. Running along the car's outside wall was the dishwasher, waist-high cabinets and an ice chest for fish. The cooking ranges were placed along the wall that separated the kitchen

Right: **Santa Fe passengers of the 1950s eagerly await their dinner.** *Below:* **A Santa Fe club car sporting a southwestern motif.**

A SHORT GLOSSARY OF DINING CAR STAFF TERMINOLOGY

Captain: The conductor.

China Cabinet: The cone-shaped strainer used for deep fat frying.

Crew's Portion: A double order of food, whether actually for a crew member or for a patron.

Del Robie: The large oval tables on both sides of the center of the dining car.

Dog House: The main refrigerator.

Doggie: An adjective describing a waiter who is not feeling well.

Dresser: The counter where vegetables are prepared.

Eyes: Block signals.

Flat: A dining car when full.

Forty-eight and standing: A full dining car. (They typically had 48 seats) with people waiting to be seated.

Getting in some time: Being lazy.

Going upstairs: Serving a meal outside the dining car. (*See Nellie*)

Nellie: A room service customer, or someone who is taking his or her meal outside the dining car.

Pearl Diver: One who washes dishes. A synonym for *Turtle*.

Putting him on the boss's desk: The process of turning in a waiter for an infraction.

Smoke Wagon: A steam locomotive.

Struggle Buggy: An old dining car.

Switch: An order to 'stop talking.'

Television: A dishwasher with a plate glass window.

The Hole: The wide shelf by which the kitchen is separated from the pantry.

Tubbing: the process of a waiter refusing to pool his tips.

Turtle: One who washes dishes. A synonym for *Pearl Diver*.

Up a tree: Condition of not knowing what one is doing.

from the corridor. Most ranges were heated by logs of compressed sawdust, although the Pennsylvania Railroad, the Illinois Central and the New Haven introduced electric ranges in the 1950s. The main refrigerator (the 'Dog House'), which was also electrified after 1945, was across the kitchen's rear side. This was the station of the second cook, who had charge of the refrigerator, salads, vegetables and baking.

The third cook, who worked next to the chef, handled steaks, chops and all food cooked on the charcoal broilers. Next came the assistant second cook. He handled egg dishes, hot cakes and potatoes. The fourth cook, who worked alongside the second cook, was in charge of the steam table and the dishwasher.

To save money, railroads started making the fourth cook a swing man. He might help serve lunch and dinner between New York and Pittsburgh, then leave the train at Pittsburgh and help serve breakfast and lunch the next day on a New York-bound train.

Dining car supervisors constantly patrolled the railroads, getting off a train heading in one direction, then boarding another one going the opposite way. They tasted the food, observed the crews' deportment and inspected standards of cleanliness. When an inspector was on the prowl, crews passed the word in several unique ways from one train to another. If an inspector got off an eastbound train at Cleveland, for example, its crew would signal all westbound trains they met. The warning might be a ketchup bottle sitting in a certain window, a waiter waving a tablecloth, a cook holding a frying pan at arm's length or a towel tied on the safety bar of the kitchen door that opened from the side of the car. When the late Major John F Trout was superintendent of the Pennsylvania's dining car service, the signal between trains that he was out on an inspection trip was a cook standing in the open door holding a large fish by the tail.

The *Twentieth Century Limited*, which considered itself a sort of club, was inhabited by 'regulars' (commuters) between Chicago and New York. Many of these expected to be recognized and catered to. The dining car staff always cited Spencer Tracy as having perhaps the strangest food habit of the many movie folk who regularly rode the *Century*. He always had a waiter awaken him at 5 am, whereupon he drank a full pot of black coffee and went back to bed. Bing Crosby often whistled and sang while going to the diner, and Morton Downey would sing all night if he could round up a barbershop quartet.

Former President Herbert Hoover liked eggs three times a day. Robert Maynard Hutchins, former president of the University of Chicago, liked his toast burnt black, and Marshall Field never ordered more than one martini, though the staff always remembered that he appeared profoundly disappointed when there was not enough remaining in the jug for a second round. The late Joseph Duveen, the legendary art dealer, would ride the train with four bodyguards and a fortune in paintings. He never

Dining on a Union Pacific Domeliner provided good food against the dramatic backdrop of the western terrain. The cutaway *(below)* shows the layout of a domeliner, while the photographs *(above)* reveal the details of the richly appointed dining rooms. Note the fine linens, china and silver.

Welcome to the
Turquoise Room

the only private dining room in the world on rails

aboard the new Super Chief

Entertain in the grand manner while en route between Chicago and Los Angeles —
in a perfectly appointed private dining room for a party up to ten.

The Turquoise Room in the new Lounge Car of the new Super Chief is the most
distinctive social feature ever provided on any train.

You are invited to enjoy it, and the other new features on the beautiful new
all-room Super Chief. For Turquoise Room reservations, just consult
any Santa Fe ticket agent, or the dining-car steward on the Super Chief

R. T. Anderson, General Passenger Traffic Manager, Santa Fe System Lines, Chicago 4, Illinois

selected his own dinner, preferring to be surprised by the steward.

Also celebrity-studded were Santa Fe's *Chief* and *Super Chief* between Chicago and Los Angeles. The Fred Harvey caterers liked to boast about how much money the dining cars lost on these trains. Unlike most other caterers, the Fred Harvey people used no frozen foods, and served prize beef, lobsters, oysters and shrimps. Orange juice was squeezed fresh to order, and strawberries, melons, fresh asparagus and fresh figs were always on the menu—in or out of season. Dairies operated by Harvey at Newton, Kansas and Las Vegas, Nevada, supplied fresh milk, cream and butter. Mountain trout were required to be so fresh their eyes still looked alive.

The *Super Chief*'s *Turquoise Room* in the car adjoining the diner was the only private dining room remaining on any regular train in the 1950s. It seated nine persons and was used for parties, dinners and business meetings by such people as Henry Ford II, Conrad Hilton and movie men Howard Dietz, Jack Cohn, Barney Balaban, Louis B Mayer and Cecil B deMille. The room was not the exclusive domain of celebrities, however. It could also be reserved by any passenger—at no extra cost—on a first-come-first-served basis.

A steward's greatest drudgery was always keeping up with taxes. Every time a train crossed a state line, the dining car department was confronted with a new tax structure. The price of a meal ordered in Illinois but eaten in Indiana had to include the Illinois tax. (A meal ordered in Indiana and consumed in Illinois had no tax.) Liquor taxes varied in almost all states. From Boston to New York, trains encountered a five percent old-age tax in Massachusetts, a two percent sales tax in Rhode Island and a three percent sales tax in Connecticut. New Jersey had no food taxes, but wouldn't let trains sell aspirin to passengers. (Only registered pharmacists could sell aspirin in New Jersey.)

Unlike the stewards, however, waiters might travel a route for years without knowing where the state lines were or even learning the names of rivers or mountains they would pass. One Santa Fe waiter used to give approximately the same reply to all questions about the names of passing landmarks. 'Those are the Johnson Mountains,' the waiter would answer, or 'the Johnson River,' or 'Johnson Mesa.' Passengers were usually satisfied, not realizing that the waiter's only authority for such statements was that his own name was Johnson.

That the dining car was the real heartbeat and life of a train is best emphasized when trains sometimes were isolated for days by upheavals of nature. In January 1952, the streamliner *City of San Francisco* was stalled in a howling blizzard in the High Sierra from noon Sunday until Wednesday. (*See accompanying photo*). For those four days, dining car activity did the most to keep morale high. The crew managed to feed some 230 persons two meals a day. By Tuesday, dinner consisted of spaghetti without sauce, a frankfurter and a half a cup of coffee per passenger. Breakfasts were a dab of canned beans, fried potatoes and coffee. The crew chopped up all the wood on the train—including Pullman ladders—to keep the cooking stoves going. These meals would not have been considered too bad by train travelers in 1880—nor indeed by some airline passengers in 1980!

Right: Snowbound in the Sierras! In January 1952, a monstrous blizzard trapped passengers aboard the *City of San Francisco* for four days. By stretching supplies and using a little ingenuity, the dining car personnel were able to feed the hungry travelers. Although the passengers were certainly a bit stir-crazy by the time rescue crews dug them out, the situation, fortunately, was never life-threatening.

Below: Great Northern's *Empire Builder* charges in from the Great Plains near its rendezvous with the Continental Divide at Marias Pass. Beginning in 1929, the luxurious *Empire Builder* ran from Chicago to Seattle. Since the 1970s, the *Empire Builder* has been operated by Amtrak.

FAREWELL TO THE RAILS

In 1955 journalist Don Eddy rode nine legendary trains on a lazy trip from California to New York and back. He crossed 22 states, visited 10 state capitals (and Washington, DC), topped the Continental Divide on a summit 10,221 feet high, rode a glass bubble through a precipitous chasm 2000 feet deep, dined regally on fresh Rocky Mountain trout, Kansas City beef, Maine lobsters and Oregon salmon, and learned a great deal about North America's railroads.

Out of his experience came the bittersweet conviction that few travelers of his day (and certianly of our own) realized the extraordinary adventure then possible on the inexhaustible choice of routes available over the nation's 295,000 miles of lines. His story bubbles with optimism which, in retrospect, is a sad tale because such a trip is not possible on AMTRAK today.

'Under a bright, full moon one night last spring, as I was tooling the old jalaop along a highway beside a railroad track across the star-spangled plains of western Nebraska, a train overtook and passed me. First, the big diesel, slick as a greased pig; then the streamlined cars, the diner glittering with silver and napery, the tern with soft lights on muraled walls, the Pullmans with porters shaking out snowy linen. Dog-tired after pounding the road full tilt all day, the sight of this easy luxury gave me a twinge of envy. But what really excited me were the bubbles.'

Don Eddy was aware that glass-topped bubble cars, variously called Vista-, Strata-or Astra-Domes, had appeared on several railroads, but this was their 'first impact' on him. 'Blowing soft blue-white above the roofs of coaches and lounge cars, they swept past eerily. I saw people up there basking in the moonlight. Long after the train left me in the lurch, I watched the parade of luminescent blobs gliding like a fleet of flying saucers across the yonder prairie.'

He called on the railrod ticket agent and asked him how he could transform a routine business trip into a vacation following 'roundabout meanderings,' going as far as possible, stopping off at points of interest—'at no higher fare than via the shortest?'

The station agent hauled out timetables and maps, drew wide circles between the coasts, and finally produced an official publication to prove an almost unbelievable statement: that there were literally tens of thousands of possible combinations of routes, perhaps as many as 100,000, the vast majority at no extra fare! This didn't include innumerable scenic side trips, most of which were then possible at little or no additional cost.

At that time, it cost less than $145 to make a roundtrip by coach between New York City and any Pacific Coast terminal (Seattle, Portland, San Francisco, Los Angeles, San Diego), or about $60 additional for first class (sleepers or parlor cars) plus Pullman charges and tax, and it cost no more to expand the roundtrip into any of thousands of big circles.

Suppose, for example, you started from New York City. One might go west via the Great Lakes, Chicago, St Paul-Minneapolis, the Dakotas, Montana, and Idaho to Seattle; skirt the Pacific Ocean southward 1500 miles to San Diego; return east along the Mexican border through the Southwest and along the Gulf Coast to New Orleans and Mobile; and angle up to New York via Atlanta, Wshington, Baltimore and Philadelphia. Furthermore, one might take six months to loop the loop if one liked stopping off whenever and wherever the 'spirit moveth.'

Eddy recalled that 'I had to see that circle on a map to comprehend how big it really was. It took in just about everything: the great inland seas, the North Woods, the Wild West, cowboys, Indians, mountains, canyons, deserts, the four greatest American cities, the fabulous Pacific Coast, Puget Sound, giant Redwoods, orange groves, Hollywood, old Spanish missions, jet airplane fields and factories, forests of Candelabra cacti, the romantic Rio Grande, the old South, cotton fields, antebellum mansions, the Evangeline country along the storied Bayou Teche, New Orleans and its Vieux Carré, plantations of sugar cane and tobacco, Mobile's exquisite Azalea Trail, both ends of the mighty Mississippi, the Gulf of Mexico, the national capital, and the home of the Liberty Bell, to mention only a few. Whew! It even included the full width of Texas and a gander at the Alamo.'

His roundtrip, starting and finishing in San Francisco, took

Below: The *City of San Francisco* winds its way around a gentle curve. *Right:* A young boy and his faithful companion wave to the engineer of a passenger train passing through Raleigh, North Carolina. Like many a boy, he probably fancies himself at the controls of a locomotive one day.

Above: Santa Fe's *San Diegan* once zoomed down the scenic California coast. Today
Amtrak handles the route.

just two weeks in traveling time, including sightseeing stop-
overs, during which time he 'met grand people, ate like a
majaraja, slept like a baby in a cradle, listened to good music
when it pleasured me and turned it off when it didn't, telephoned
the boss (collect, natch!) from a barber chair while having my
hair cut on a train going 79 miles an hour, exercised my low
Dutch on a party of German statesmen who had no idea what I
was talking about (which made it unanimous), dictated letters to
a traveling public secretary for free, swished around mountain
grades so twisty the locomotive was sometimes behind the cars
it was pulling, and learned how to keep coffee from sloshing out
of a cup when the train hits a sharp curve.'

The *California Zephyr*, the same train that Don Eddy had seen
weeks before in Nebraska, was spectacularly streamlined, with
five Vista-Domes. Jointly owned and operated by the Burlington, Rio Grande and Western Pacific railroads, the *California Zephyr* then plied the rails between Chicago and Oakland,
with a through sleeper to New York.

His seatmate in the sunny Vista-Dome was a young man with
'a big bump of curiosity and a completely charming candor.' He
was Tommy Poe, aged 12, of Arlington, Virginia, younger son of
Edgar A Poe, a Washington newspaperman. It developed that
the Poe family—Ed, Frances, their son Edgar, 18, and
Tommy—were on a 7000-mile railroad vacation which, Tommy
assured him, 'hadn't overlooked a thing.'

'On a Santa Fe train,' Eddy noted, 'Tommy had powwowed
with a real, live Indian chief thoughtfully provided by the
management. In Hollywood, he had been hugged by a movie
star. He had dunked in the Pacific and climbed a mountain. He
was loaded with souvenirs and memories and had learned more
geography than he could ever have gotten from books.'

In the early afternoon, the *California Zephyr* bored into one of
the Far West's wonderlands, the Feather River Canyon, for the
long ascent of the Sierra Nevada. 'I had driven through it many
times,' Eddy recalled, 'but I never really saw the famous canyon
until that day in the Vista-Dome. From the glass walls, the view
was unobstructed—the creaming river beside the tracks, the
lofty evergreen slopes and craggy ramparts soaring to the blue
wedge of sky far above. But Tommy wanted to go exploring, so
we wandered through the train.'

Tommy noticed a peculiar, fencelike string of wires beside the
tracks and asked what it was. Don Eddy couldn't tell him, but 63-
year-old veteran trainman WD 'Stubby' Kelly had the answer.

'It's a slide detector,' Kelly explained. 'If a rock slid down the
mountain it would break one of those wires before reaching the

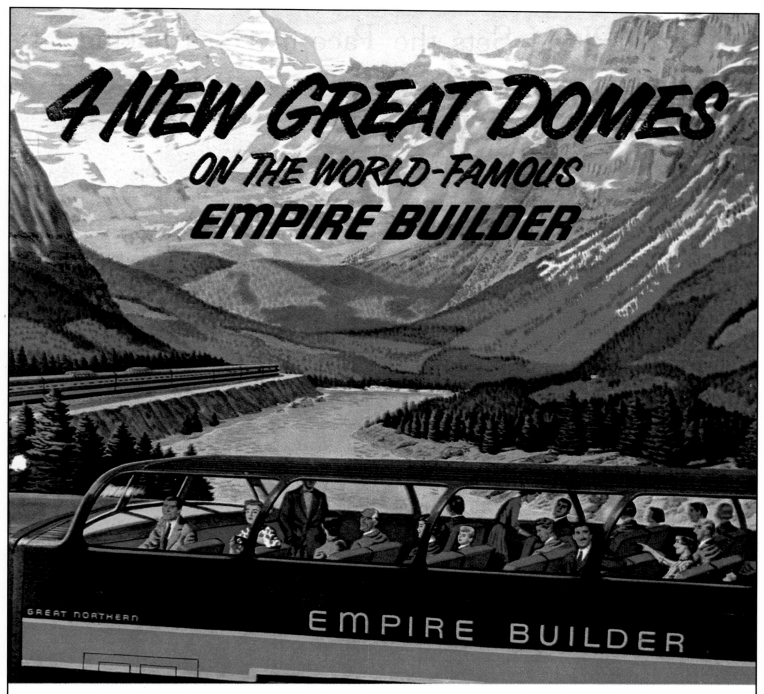

4 NEW GREAT DOMES
ON THE WORLD-FAMOUS
EMPIRE BUILDER

GREAT NORTHERN

EMPIRE BUILDER

MORE LUXURY DOME SEATS FOR THE MOST SCENIC MILES ON ANY TRAIN BETWEEN CHICAGO·TWIN CITIES·SPOKANE·SEATTLE·PORTLAND

GO GREAT...GO GREAT NORTHERN

There now are 147 topside seats in the Great Domes on the distinguished Empire Builder—the most dome seats on any streamliner between Chicago and Pacific Northwest cities. And, there's *no extra fare* for helping yourself to a grandstand seat for the *extra wonderful sightseeing* in Great Northern country. Three luxurious Great Domes in the coach section of the Empire Builder, plus an exciting, colorful full-length Great Dome in the Pullman section, with a smart lounge on the lower deck. Go Great Northern—and you'll go great!

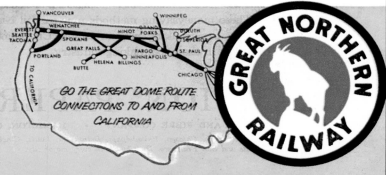

GO THE GREAT DOME ROUTE
CONNECTIONS TO AND FROM
CALIFORNIA

GREAT NORTHERN RAILWAY

For information: Write Passenger Dept., Great Northern, St. Paul 1, Minn.

rails and every train would stop automatically until the line was inspected and cleared.'

A myriad of such safety devices helped to account for the railroads' remarkable safety record of fewer than one fatality in the equivalent of 100,000 roundtrips coast to cast. It was a record that is matched tenfold by the airlines today, but not by the airlines in the early 1950s and before.

The recorded musical programs over the public address system during the day had been interrupted occasionally by a liting feminine voice announcing sights of interest. Finally, Don Eddy and Tommy met the voice herself, the *Zephyrette*, Virginia Lovejoy of East Hampton, New York, the only woman among the 33 members of the crew. Her dad, Commodore Ferold D Lovejoy, was then a Navy doctor in the Far East. 'We're both getting paid to see the world,' she remarked with a twinkle.

At Tommy's insistence, Eddy decided to stop over in Salt Lake City, Utah with the Poes the next day. Only a minute was required for conductor John Fletcher to rearrange his ticket. 'It's good on any railroad going in the right direction,' he said amiably. 'No trouble at all. Been doing it for 42 years. Have a good time.'

At bedtime, Don Eddy got acquainted with his roomette, a compact, private room with 'all the conveniences of home.' Already made up, the bed was hidden in the wall. He lowered it

The 1950s-era passenger trains had something for every-one—in the corner of the observation car, a friendly card game could be found (*left*) or you could relax with family and friends as ever-changing vistas rolled by (*above*). Best of all, from high atop the dome, you could enjoy the spectacular panorama of the Rockies (*at top*).

Right: A Union Pacific advertisement for Domeliners promised 'pleasant relaxation' in their lounge and club cars, and these passengers aboard the UP's *Challenger (above)* would certainly agree with that claim. In their glory days, domeliners made traveling to one's destination as much fun as the vacation itself!

'with a flick of the wrist, tucked myself in, turned off the lights, softened the music, raised the window shade and watched the lights of automobiles racing across the Nevada desert. Travel by train, I decided drowsily, was a lot easier.'

After a sightseeing tour of Salt Lake City, Don Eddy boarded the Rio Grande's *Royal Gorge* the next afternoon as the sun's last rays were 'painting the Wasatch Mountains.' Just 745 miles across the backbone of the continent, the Rockies, lay his next goal, the 'Queen City of the Plains,' Denver.

Like the *California Zephyr*, the *Royal Gorge* sported a Vista-Dome. This was particularly appropriate, for it was in the Rocky Mountains that the idea of an observation dome was conceived on a July day in 1944 by CR Osborn, vice president of General Motors. Riding in the glass nose of a diesel, it struck him that a glass-topped passenger car would be popular. It was just a year later when the first Vista-Dome went into service on the Chicago, Burlington & Quincy, and today a monument still stands beside the tracks where Mr Osborn had his hot flash.

When Don Eddy went to sleep that night a pale moon was glimmering on the tumbling Colorado River, westbound to Boulder Dam and the Gulf of California. When he awakened he was on the roof of the continent, Tennessee Pass, 10,240 feet high, and sunrise was pinkening an eastbound river, the Arkansas, headed for the Mississippi. As he breakfasted, breathless vistas unfolded at every turn of the wheels. Far to the south, the snowy minarets of the Sangre de Cristo range were scarlet in the early light, just as Spanish explorers first saw them and named them Blood of Christ. Then, in midmorning, the train dipped into the big thrill of this route for which the train is named—the mystic Royal Gorge.

The Vista-Dome was the place to enjoy it. Don Eddy noted, without fear of contradiciton, 'The brightly colored canyon walls closed in, soaring until they seemed almost to meet half a mile straight up, and the floor of the gorge was bathed in eerie rose-tinted shadow. Where the train stopped, you could flip pebbles from one wall to the other. A fifth of a mile overhead, a dark thread against the sky marked an engineering marvel, the world's highest highway bridge. Even voluble young Tommy Poe was speechless with awe.'

East of the gorge the train began to catch distant glimpses of Pikes Peak, most famous of the Rocky Mountains (although 27 are higher), and it was still visible when the *Royal Gorge* pulled into Denver, where Don Eddy reluctantly parted from the Poes. They were continuing eastward on a leisurely route. Eddy who

had 'worked up an itch to ride a railroad cannonball'—one of the world's fastest trains—headed to the Uniion Pacific's *City of Denver*. He boarded it the next afternoon and was sipping a sarsaparilla in the pub, a handsome wood-paneled taproom on wheels, when the train took off.

In an automobile, the driver of the 1950s—not unlike the driver of the 1990s—would be satisfied to average 50 miles per hour for a day's run. On the *City of Denver* Don Eddy rode 560 miles in eight hours, an average of 70 mph, a good speed, even on today's interstates. 'Scenery flashed past in a blur; the station agent's garden beside the Julesburg depot, where flowers bloomed between rows of corn; seas of ripening wheat; miles of beets and of factories converting them into sugar; the Rockies dwindling on the far horizon as we whipped across the Great Plains, until at last they were only a violet haze lined in gold against the setting sun.'

Steward Benjamin F Merriman of Chicago was the happiest man on the train that day. He had just heard a rumor that the *City of Denver* would soon have the newest thing in observation cars—an Astra-Dome diner, the first in America and one of 35 new Astra-Domes then being added to Union Pacific streamliners. Don Eddy was personally more excited by the fact that Steward Merriman could *telephone the engineer* and keep him posted on their speed as he ate dinner. With the chicken soup came the first bulletin: 75.8 mph. With the salad, 77.4 mph. With the grilled mountain trout, 79.2 mph. Finally, with the strawberry shortcake, and for 95 miles thereafter, the *City of Denver's* speed never dropped below 80 mph.

Observation-lounge car on the famous
PANAMA LIMITED

This luxurious Illinois Central train is powered by a General Motors Diesel locomotive on its daily 16½-hour run, 921 miles each way between Chicago and New Orleans. Also powered by GM Diesels are the I.C.'s other famous trains—City of New Orleans, City of Miami, Green Diamond, Daylight, Night Diamond, Land O'Corn and Miss Lou.

"Ninety-five? I thought we were doing about sixty!"

Unless you count the mileposts as they flash by, you can hardly believe the distance the Panama Limited is covering with a General Motors Diesel locomotive up at the head of the train.

The flow of power is so smooth that you get from here to there almost before you know it, at a hundred miles an hour a lot of the time.

The Panama Limited is just one example of how GM Diesel locomotives have stepped up schedules on American railroads.

Throughout the country, there are at least 96 different runs made from start to stop at 60 miles or more — a total of more than 7,320 daily scheduled miles. There are more than 23 non-stop runs of 102 to 325 miles in length covered at averages of 60 to 80 miles an hour.

This stepping up of schedules is one of the benefits which GM Diesel locomotives have brought to more than 150 famous name trains on more than a score of railroads — and that is just about all of the Diesel-powered crack trains in the United

States. And in addition, these GM Diesel locomotives are so reliable that some railroads report as high as 97% "on time" arrivals.

No wonder more and more of the crack trains of the nation are being powered by these General Motors locomotives.

In the thirteen years since they first made their bow, they have helped the railroads reduce operating costs — and increased passenger traffic, because they made train travel such a pleasure.

"Better trains follow better locomotives"

ELECTRO-MOTIVE DIVISION

GENERAL MOTORS

LA GRANGE, ILL.

GM GENERAL MOTORS

DIESEL POWER

As the *City of Denver* headed on to Chicago, Don Eddy dropped off at Omaha that evening for a 'gabfest' with old friends. Before noon next day, though, he boarded 'another speedball,' the Rock Island Lines' *Corn Belt Rocket*, for the 493-mile dash to the Windy City in nine hours flat. It was a conductor on the *Corn Belt Rocket* who taught Eddy how to keep coffee from sloshing out of a cup. 'Put a spoon in it,' he advised. 'If that doesn't work, use two spoons.' One did the trick.

After a night in Chicago, Don Eddy boarded one of the most famous of America's crack trains, the New York Central's *Twentieth Century Limited*, for the 961-mile sprint to New York City. In 1955 the *Twentieth Century Limited* sometimes had to run in several sections to handle the crowds, but on its first run, in 1902, it had only three Pullmans and 27 passengers. Even then, it had a barber-valet and a public stenographer, and it was one of the few trains to maintain those services into the 1950s. It also had private rooms with a shower bath.

When Eddy found the barbershop, that was the end. He plopped into the chair. He chatted with the tonsorialist, ER Miller of Tinley Park, Illinois, while he mowed Eddy's 'curly tresses.'

'Yes,' Miller said, 'I've worked on capitalists, politicians, gangsters and theatrical stars during my 15 years on the railroads. I've charged them all the same—haircut $1.25, shave 85 cents.'

'Do those big wheels tip loosely?,' Eddy asked Miller.

'Well,' he said, 'yes and no. They don't throw their money around. Sometimes two dollars, or even three, but usually about a dollar.'

Eddy settled sheepishly for 50 cents.

As he was preparing to leave, the train secretary, Andrew Henry of Chicago, came in from his office next door. He was both stenographer and telephone operator, and there was no charge for his services. Like the car phones of the 1980s, the telephone on the *Twentieth Century Limited* operated by radio to the nearest mobile exchange, then by wire and wireless to all the world. 'People call up the darndest places,' Henry told Eddy. 'Teheran, Luxembourg, Mozambique. They even telephone ships in midocean to kid their friends.'

Among Henry's biggest thrills of his 32 years on the *Century* was the time when the White House telephoned a passenger. One of the high spots was taking dictation from President Coolidge. 'Didn't take long,' Henry observed dryly. 'Mr Collidge had what you might call a paucity of conversation.'

The *Century*'s approach to New York City was down the broad Hudson River from Albany, past hamlets where great deeds were done in revolutionary times, making it one of America's most fascinating trips. Then, of course, few experiences could compare with the arrival at Grand Central Station: 'The long march past crowds gathered to watch this celebrated train pull in, the rotunda with sunlight slanting through its tall window, the grand staircase with its hyrring throngs, the impatient bah and roar of taxicabs shuttling in and out of the cavernous driveways like hornets from a hive.'

For the first train of his return to the West Coast, Don Eddy picked the Baltimore & Ohio's streamlined *Capitol Limited*. Although the B & O was America's oldest commercial railroad, its tracks did not run into New York City, so Eddy had no problem with crowds, taxicabs or redcaps. He merely stepped outside his hotel and into one of the big buses in which the railroad picked up passengers all around the city. They rolled comfortably through Times Square, Greenwich Village, along the docks under the very prows of moored ocean liners, and onto

The Magic Carpet rolls out again

IT'S CENTURY TIME! A minute ago, outside the station, you were in the heart of a great city, with hurrying crowds, blaring taxis, newsboys shouting the evening headlines. Now you're in a different world as you follow that crimson carpet down the platform of Grand Central Terminal toward the softly lighted, streamlined cars that will be your club on wheels for tonight.

Relax by Twilight

Magically, the day's tension vanishes when you step into the Century's luxurious Observation car. Deep cushioned easy chairs invite you to relax. And outside the wide windows, the twilit beauty of the Water Level Route unrolls a background for repose.

The Face is Familiar

Beside superb cuisine and service, there's a fascination about dinner on this favorite train of famous people. For nearby may be a lovely face you last saw in technicolor, or a distinguished one that would be news on any financial page.

Awake Refreshed

You arrive looking and feeling your best. For all night, in the quiet privacy of your room, a spacious bed, a rubber-foam mattress, and the smooth Water Level Route have conspired to give you deep, refreshing sleep.

NEW YORK CENTRAL
The Water Level Route—You Can Sleep

The *only* all-room extra-fare train between New York and Chicago.

20TH CENTURY LIMITED

a B & O ferry, one of 1800 ships operated by the nation's railroads.

As they shoved off, the passing *Queen Mary* honked companionably at the tiny ferry and it honked right back. The ferry docked in New Jersey, the bus rolled straight through the terminal and out beside the tracks, stopping at the entrance to Eddy's car. 'That, I thought, was tops in service,' he recalled.

Great American history was made along the route over which he rode in air-conditioned luxury that day: Philadelphia, where Betsy Ross designed the Stars and Stripes and where the Liberty Bell is enshrined in Independence Hall; Washington, its stately buildings and monuments symbolizing freedom throughout the world; Harper's Ferry, where three states and two rivers meet in the Blue Ridge Mountains of West Virginia, and where John Brown's savage raid in 1859 cut the pattern for the War Between the States. At Washington, the *Capitol Limited* picked up a private car of Detroit high school students headed home after one of the all-expense-paid student tours for which the B & O was once famous.

After dark that night, the *Capitol Limited* observation car, called a Strata-Dome, sprang a surprise—a powerful floodlight to illuminate the scenery. 'It was fascinating to sit under the stars and watch vignettes of countryside whirl through the path of light,' Eddy remembered. 'I was still up there when our floodlight was paled by the Mephistophelian glare of Pittsburgh's sprawling steel mills.'

Few regions in the United States had better train service during rail travel's halcyon century than the stretch between Chicago and the Twin Cities of Minneapolis and St Paul, Minnesota. Streamliners once raced one another back and forth all around the clock. Don Eddy selected one with a 'king-sized' observation car—the Milwaukee Road's *Olympian Hiawatha*, which plied the route between Chicago and the Pacific Northwest. The *Olympian Hiawatha* had an economy-priced sleeper called Touralux, a streamlined version of the old-time tourist car. Another innovation was a spacious, rear-end, glass-domed observation section called a Skytop Lounge. The highlight of the train, however, was its observation car, called a Super-Dome, twice the size of most such cars, with 68 seats upstairs over a swanky lounge-cafe.

As the *Olympian Hiawatha* rolled past Milwaukee's lovely parks and on past lakes with such sneezy names as Pewaulkee, Nagawicka and Okauchee, the bartender 'puddled me a pleasing potion of potent pabulum and bragged about his train,' Don Eddy mused poetically.

'Each window upstairs cost $400,' the bartender told him. 'The two cars cost half a million. The train itself, one of several sisters, cost $1.5 million, and it is only one of some 650 "name" trains on American lines.'

'This luxury,' Eddy reflected, 'accounts for some of the United States railroads' $33 billion capital investment—owned, incidentally, by 835,000 stockholders.'

Eddy had a night and a day in the Twin Cities, and then, as the crisp nothern twilight closed down, he boarded his eighth train, the Northern Pacific Railway's deluxe *North Coast Limited*, for the longest continuous ride of his great circle, a ride which would carry him two-thirds of the width of the continent along the Main Street of the Northwest in a day and a half.

'I thought I had seen everything in the way of observation cars,' he recollected,' but the *North Coast Limited* had something brand new—a Vista-Dome sleeping car, first of its kind ever built. It is, in fact effect, a glorified upstairs sun deck for the occupants of 12 private rooms on the first floor—of whom, I am delighted to report, I was one. For an old blacktop beater like me,

Coming ... a new service to Vacationland

Olympian Hiawathas CHICAGO — PACIFIC NORTHWEST

SUMMER will bring a new transcontinental Speedliner service. You can go, on faster schedules, to Yellowstone ... western dude ranches ... Spokane's lakes and Grand Coulee Dam ... Mt. Rainier, Mt. Baker and other Puget Sound attractions centering around Seattle and Tacoma.

All equipment for the new OLYMPIAN HIAWATHAS, except the all-room sleeping cars, will be ready. This includes the roomy, angle-seating dining car and the distinctive

Tip Top Grill ... *Touralux* sleeping cars that bring new luxury with economy ... famous Hiawatha Luxury Lounge coaches that are even further improved.

Free Vacation Information

For literature on vacations in the Northwest Wonderland via the OLYMPIAN HIAWATHAS, write F. N. Hicks, Passenger Traffic Manager, The Milwaukee Road, 722 Union Station, Chicago 6, Illinois.

THE MILWAUKEE ROAD

it was utter luxury to sit up there in my sunshine with my morning coffee and my newspaper, listening to soft music and watching the scenery unfold hour after hour—while somebody else did the driving. This, I decided, was something that should happen to me more often.'

By early spring 1956, there would be four Vista-Domes on each *North Coast Limited*, two of them on sleepers, part of a $7.5 million passenger improvement program even then in progress on the Northern Pacific. However, it would never be completed. By 1970, this luxury passenger service was gone and the Northern Pacific name was lost in a merger with the Burlington. The grand Vista-Dome that had once given so much pleasure to passengers and pride to its company ended it's traveling days rusting on a railyard siding while it waited for the scrap man's torch.

Don Eddy's ninth train during the summer of 1955 was the Southern Pacific's sumptuous *Shasta Daylight*. It rushed 718 miles between Portland and San Francisco through scenery possibly unsurpassed in the Far West. As Eddy described his initial encounter with the ultra-modern train: 'When the porter took my suitcase, he didn't carry it into the car, he set it on a built-in elevator and it whooshed up to a storage space. When I touched the door of the car, it jumped open all by itself, closing sedately after he had passed inside. When I looked for an ashtray, there it was right under my hand. It was like magic.'

The diner was another innovation—not one car long, but three cars invisibly connected. One was the kitchen, one a formal

UNWITTING PROPHECY

If several Eastern railroads have their way with the Interstate Commerce Comission, minimum rail sleeping accommodations from New York to Chicago will soon cost $76.50. (The present fare is $55.25. A first-class New York-to-Chicago plane ticket is now $49.61.)

Six roads asked on 10 August for a 45 percent increase in Pullman fares and a five percent rise in coach tariffs. If the idea is to price Pullman accommodations out of existence, they are assuredly going about it in the very best way.

There are thousands of persons who, given the mobility of US life, must travel long distances at considerable inconvenience and great personal expense to themselves. Often these persons are elderly or sick. They don't care to fly; they cannot drive their own cars; they are unable to sustain the rigors of bus travel. It is too much to ask them to sit (or stand) in what are often crowded, smoke-filled railroad coaches. For these thousands, Pullman accommodations are a necessity, not a luxury.

Railroads, we realize, get their profits from freight, not passengers. We regret that their annual losses on passenger service have been so great. But if they cannot provide reasonably priced sleeping accommodations for Eastern travelers, then—in view of the common good—it will perhaps be necessary for the government to take over and subsidize what used to be one of the symbols of private enterprise. No one is going to like to see that happen.

—America Magazine
25 August 1956

Left: **Southern Pacific's fabled *Shasta Daylight* plies the rugged Cascades on a moody Monday morning.**

dining room, one an informal coffee shop. Eddy recalled being almost afraid to look at the prices on the menu, but they were about the same as he had found on other trains, comparable to good restaurants 'ashore.' Complete breakfasts ran from $1.20 to $1.80, lucheons and dinners from $1.70 to $2.15. When he complimented instructing chef William Whitley on the fluffiness of an omelette, he said, 'You ought to try my wife's omlettes.'

'She must be a good cook,' Eddy replied, to which Whitley grinned.

'Well, in 31 years, I should have been able to teach her a few things. When she wants to wheedle me, she makes fried chicken marinated, simmered and smothered in a sauce of white wine, onions and mushrooms.'

The windows on the *Shasta Daylight* were the largest Eddy had yet seen on any train. They were appreciated, for the route ran through a wonderland. Each mile had its own vignette: 'Lumberjacks birling nimbly on logs in midriver... the elegant monument to a cow near Marion, Oregon... the crossing of the Cascades, snowy crests piled range on range like waves of a celestial sea... a lonely cabin clinging to a cliff in a primeval forest... a hairpin turn where the engine twists bebehind the observation car... snow-white pelicans on the shallows of an ancient inland ocean... Mt Shasta's frozen cone under its snowy mantle... the shattered peak of the still active volcano Mt Lassen... golden pheasants scurrying for cover in the Sacramento Valley, and black clouds of wild fowl beating up from flooded

The last sunset. Southern Pacific's grand San Francisco station *(above)* was demolished in the 1970s. *Right:* Night 'comes in a-falling.'

rice fields. They were pictures to remember.'

The final stop on Eddy's tour was the man-made Oakland Mole that thrust a mile out into San Francisco Bay. The ferry was there. The great Bay Bridge was 'etched in dots of light against the stars, and over on the yonder shore the myriad bright windows were shining on the everlasting hills of San Francisco. My trip was ended... '

Don Eddy found the choice of available routes to be amazing. 'If all the railroad lines in America were sketched on a map you wouldn't be able to see the map.' He also was amazed by the 'ease of it, with nothing to do but loaf and eat and sleep while other people do the work.' He noted, too, the dependability and safety of it. 'No train I rode was more than three minutes late, and it never occurred to me to worry about getting there in one piece. These things add up to a log of solid satisfaction. Would I do it again? Let's don't be silly. When do we start?'

It seemed like a choice that would be available forever, but soon it would not be, and the Don Eddys of the 1960s, 1970s, 1980s and 1990s would squeeze into tiny seats beside the tiny windows of airliners for their trip across America.

America. For the most part, it can now sadly be said, 'The train doesn't go there any more.'

THE END

INDEX

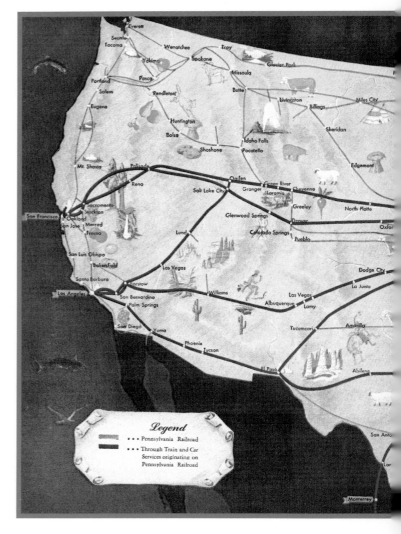

RAILROAD LADY
by Jimmy Buffett and Jerry Jeff Walker

She's a railroad lady, just a little bit shady,
Spending her days on the train.
She's a semi-good looker, but the fast rails they took her;
Now she's tryin', just tryin' to get home again.

From South Station in Boston, to the stockyards of Austin;
From the Florida sunshine, to the New Orleans rain;
And now that the Rail PACs have taken the best tracks;
She's tryin', just tryin' to get home again.

She's a railroad lady, just a little bit shady,
Spending her life on the trains.
Once a Pullman car traveler, now the brakeman won't have her;
She's tryin', just tryin' to get home again.

Once a highballing loner, he thought he could own her,
He bought her a fur coat and a big diamond ring.
She hocked them for cold cash and left town on the Wabash;
Not thinking, never thinking of home, way back then.

But the rails are now rusty; the dining car's dusty;
The gold plated watches have taken their toll.
The railroads are dying, and the lady, she's crying
On a bus to Kentucky and home, that's her goal.